AN EXPERIMENTAL MANUAL IN PSYCHOLOGY

BY

JOHN FREDERICK DASHIELL

PROFESSOR OF PSYCHOLOGY
THE UNIVERSITY OF NORTH CAROLINA

HOUGHTON MIFFLIN COMPANY

BOSTON · NEW YORK · CHICAGO · DALLAS
ATLANTA · SAN FRANCISCO
The Riverside Press Cambridge

The Riverside Press
CAMBRIDGE · MASSACHUSETTS
PRINTED IN THE U.S.A.

PREFACE

PSYCHOLOGY, long considered dependent for her factual material upon the empirical procedures of natural science, is becoming increasingly recognized as a branch of human knowledge that must also be *taught* in a natural science spirit. If students are to have any adequate appreciation of psychological principles, they must have first-hand knowledge of investigative methods, experimental, statistical, and clinical, most especially the first.

For beginning students the experimental courses are in many institutions becoming incorporated with the more theoretical lecture-and-textbook courses; in other places they still have the status of follow-up work with cross-references to theoretical principles presented in the preceding courses.

This manual is primarily designed for the use of the beginning experimental work, on either of these plans. It is the outgrowth of the author's pedagogical experiments extending over some years, in the teaching of an introductory two-semester course. It will be found, however, that the manual is adaptable to the needs of more advanced classes, in which the more elaborate forms of apparatus and more intensive technique are to be recommended.

Many of the experiments ("individual") are arranged for students working in pairs (as experimenter and subject). A few that involve more delicate apparatus or previous experience in technique are planned as group work with an instructor in charge, but with the individual students participating in an active way. Many experiments also are planned for use in those institutions in which at present individual laboratory work is impossible, and the group procedure is to be resorted to perforce. Finally, a few exercises have been included that are not precisely experimental in character but yet are types of work demanded in scientific laboratories; such as the making of drawings, the administration of testing methods, etc.

The MANUAL was originally planned to be used in conjunction with the author's FUNDAMENTALS OF OBJECTIVE PSYCHOLOGY. The experiments parallel throughout the presentation of topics in the FUNDAMENTALS, leaving no important principles in the text without appropriate concrete approach by the student. Thus is avoided the usual disjointed and out-of-step relationship between principle and experiment, with its overemphasis on a few topics and no attention at all to others of recognized importance. The author has sought to provide the student with something concrete and

PREFACE

methodological bearing upon every one, without omission, of those principles in the FUNDAMENTALS that are to be held of first significance.

At the same time, the author believes that the selection of experiments included here makes the MANUAL as useful to teachers employing a wide variety of textbooks as a single manual can be expected to be. He has, therefore, followed the student's instructions for each experiment with suggestive reading references in representative texts.

The convenience of the instructor is held paramount. A considerable number of experiments are included so that he may more readily find those most appropriate to his material facilities, and to his personal lines of emphasis. Alternative procedures and numerous discussion questions are introduced for the same purpose. Explicit directions to the student are furnished, which can be amended and adapted where desired. Bibliographies are omitted (they can be found in the textbooks used), except that the instructor is directed to a few chosen references where he will get definite help in arranging each experiment.

In any scientific field, experiments, like theoretical principles, may become so widely used and universally accepted that an attempt to acknowledge all the sources in every instance would burden the pages and appear pedantic. Where an experiment is included in this MANUAL that is definitely traceable to a certain source or sources, the references and the implied acknowledgments are listed in the appropriate place among the NOTES FOR INSTRUCTORS.

The writer is indebted for advice and assistance in many places to Dr. A. G. Bayroff, Dr. K. L. Barkley, and Mr. H. N. DeWick, past or present instructors in the North Carolina laboratory. In preparation of the manuscript he has had the assistance of Miss Ruth Hamill and Miss Blanche Zorn. Acknowledgment is made to the C. A. Stoelting Company for permission to print illustrations of some of their apparatus.

GENERAL INSTRUCTIONS TO THE STUDENT

THE essence of a scientific experiment on any phenomenon is to control all the conditions (so far as possible), keeping all constant but one; then to vary that one to observe what other phenomena change with it (as cause, or effect, or co-effect). This logic will underly all your experiments. Look for it.

Remember that experimenting on human nature is a more complicated matter than experimenting on frogs or on hydrogen, because a human being is affected by many more kinds of influences, and so the conditions of the phenomenon being studied are much harder to control. Be on the lookout always for factors that may enter in to render your results unreliable — factors of apparatus, of procedure, of personal attitude or condition — and where they cannot be eliminated they should be included in your discussion.

In the individual experiments two students will work together, one acting as the subject (S) on whom the experiment is to be performed, the other acting as the experimenter (E). The procedure is usually repeated after the two have exchanged rôles. Thus, each student will have data on, and is to write up, the other person as his subject. In the group experiments the instructor (I) will usually serve as the principal E, and either all the individual members of the group-as-a-whole or else some selected individual, will act as S. In some group experiments the student will obtain his data at first-hand, in others indirectly from material posted on blackboard or bulletin or else mounted under glass for his inspection and measurement.

To draw a graph: Use cross-ruled paper. Lay out on it the two axes at right angles, a base or horizontal line (abscissa) and a vertical line (ordinate), with their intersection in the lower left-hand corner of the paper. Let distances on the base line represent equal units of the standard or known variable (years of age, number of practice periods, etc.), and distances on the vertical line the found values of the variable you are investigating that correspond to the units on base line (as amount of memory ability at each age given or amount learned at each practice period given). Choose such scales for the axes that the data to be represented will reach from the intersection point almost to the limits of both axes; i.e., cover as nearly as possible the whole sheet. The sheet may be used either horizontally or vertically.

Place scale numbers along both axes, writing them horizontally, and parallel with each axis write the name and units of the variable plotted along this axis. To represent your experimental data locate points at the appropriate distances in the form of large dots, then connect these dots by lines drawn with a ruler. Print neatly the name of the curve (what it shows) in a large unused portion of the sheet. Use ink throughout. There are many curves in the textbooks showing these and other points.

To time short intervals if a stop watch is not available: Use a watch with a second hand. Start the experiment when the second hand is exactly at 60 (noting also the position of minute hand) and at the end of the work note both hands again.

In writing up an experiment follow, as far as possible, the following headings:

PROBLEM: Under this heading state concisely and clearly the nature of the question supposed to be attacked in the experiment. Make clear both the general field of psychology which is involved and the particular points which are specifically attacked.

MATERIALS: Enumerate the pieces of apparatus and other materials used. In some cases a sketch will help. Sketch all electric, pneumatic, or other connections essential to a set-up.

PROCEDURE: Abbreviate the instructions given on these sheets, making your description the simplest possible general statement of what is done. If your actual procedure deviates in any way, describe it as it was *done* by *you*.

RESULTS: Here is required the greatest care. It is absolutely essential that you report exactly what you actually did get, unbiased by what you think you should have gotten. If you wish to discuss the latter do it under DISCUSSION below. Data should be taken down in permanent form and turned in with the formal report. To be scientific, results should be obtained in *quantitative* terms as far as possible. Where tables are used, keep your columns straight by using ruled lines.

DISCUSSION: Give explicit answers to all questions. Be a psychologist here: Make inferences from your experimental work, and especially connect it up with principles found in lectures or text, but beware of mere talk and of too free-and-easy a handling of psychological terms! Feel free to criticize the method or results of the experiment, especially as to sources of error. Don't make this part of the report too mechanical, but think in it.

The ideal of an experimental report is to describe so completely and accurately the experiment performed that any other scientist can know precisely what was done and what results were obtained, and can, if he desires, *repeat* the experiment for purposes of verification. Follow this ideal.

The student should obtain, in quantities specified by the instructor, the following materials: ruled paper, of composition or note-book type; data sheets, i.e., ruled paper with vertical rulings about 2 cm. for tabulations; coördinate paper, preferably mm. scale; plain bond, for drawings; cardboard for backs; and, if available, title sheets. All sheets should be punched for staples, which are also to be obtained. The data sheets are of great convenience, and should always be brought to any experimental session. If unobtainable [1] in printed form the title sheets should be made out by the student as follows:

University of ....
Psychological Laboratory
Report on
(name of experiment)
....
Submitted by
....

Experimenter......................   Subject...........................
Date performed....................   Date report due...................
Course............................   Section...........................
Time spent in writing..............   Grade.............................

Your instructor may ask for "informal" reports on certain experiments. In this case, you will clip out the statements of PROBLEM, MATERIALS, and PROCEDURE given in the MANUAL, paste them into your report with notes on any variations from them you have used, and present your full original data, adding only whatever Discussion is specified by the instructor.

Following the instructions for each experiment will be given a list of reading references to representative textbooks. Full titles for these books are given in the list below; throughout the rest of the MANUAL they will be referred to by the authors' names only:

Breese, B. B., *Psychology* (Scribners).

Dashiell, J. F., *Fundamentals of Objective Psychology* (Houghton Mifflin).

Gates, A. I., *Elementary Psychology*, Revised (Macmillan).

Hunter, W. S., *Human Behavior* (University of Chicago Press).

Perrin, F. A. C., and Klein, D. B., *Psychology* (Holt).

Pillsbury, W. B., *Fundamentals of Psychology*, Revised (Macmillan).

[1] It is best to have a local stationer supply the student with these materials assembled in a large envelope, the title sheets to be printed by him and included.

GENERAL INSTRUCTIONS TO THE STUDENT

Robinson, E. S., and Robinson, F. R., *Readings in General Psychology*, 2d edition (University of Chicago Press).

Titchener, E. B., *Text-Book of Psychology* (Macmillan).

Warren, H. C., and Carmichael, L., *Elements of Human Psychology* (Houghton Mifflin).

Watson, J. B., *Psychology from the Standpoint of a Behaviorist*, 2d edition (Lippincott).

Woodworth, R. S., *Psychology*, Revised (Holt).

LIST OF EXPERIMENTS

LIST OF EXPERIMENTS

I. LOCALIZATION OF SOUNDS: A SAMPLE PSYCHOLOGICAL EXPERIMENT (INDIVIDUAL OR GROUP)

Problem: To analyze some of the factors that are involved in perceiving the direction of a sound; i.e., in making a correct response to a stimulus-complex of spatial character.

Materials: Sound cage. (Common chair and tin "snapper" may be substituted.)

Procedure: For reading data, draw two large circles on the blackboard with 45-degree divisions indicated and the degrees marked on the outside of the circles. One circle is to be used to record directions in the subject's *sagittal* plane (a plane bisecting the body between the eyes), the other in his *horizontal* plane. Students are to copy the circles.

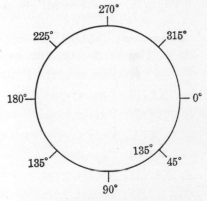

S is to sit with eyes closed and head maintained in a fixed position (by head rest). I or E is to sound sounder once at a point in the imaginary plane bisecting S's body corresponding to one of the points marked on the record circle. S is to judge the direction of the sound by pointing his finger or a pencil, his hand being held close to his chest out of E's way. E is to observe the direction indicated and is to note it in degrees upon

The figure shows one of the two record circles in which E has recorded the fact that when the sound was produced at a point corresponding to the point marked "45°," S pointed in the direction corresponding to the point marked "135°."

the inside of the record circle just opposite the point of *actual* stimulation. (Students to copy.) This is to be repeated for each of the points on the circle, in irregular order, the sounder to be held at a constant distance, about three feet, from the mid-point between the two ears.

Using the horizontal plane (on a level with S's ears), the procedure is to be repeated.

Repeat on two more individuals as S's, to compare results.

A variation in procedure may then be introduced, S cupping his hands to form "ears" turned backward.

Results: Show by reproducing the two circles and the actual and estimated directions.

Discussion:

1. Is localization more accurate in one plane than in the other?
2. Suggest two explanations of this.
3. What would be the result (or results) of producing simultaneously two sounds of identical attributes, one at 40 degrees right, and the other at 40 degrees left on horizontal plane?
4. Is the sound the only stimulus acting upon S, and is his pointing at it the only response being made by him? Be explicit! If there are other stimuli and responses involved in the totality of behavior, how are they "controlled" or checked in this experimental procedure?
5. In S's perceiving the direction of sound is the interpretative process highly conscious, vaguely conscious, or unconscious? i.e., is S clearly, vaguely, or not at all aware of the cues that guide his perceiving?

References: Dashiell, 39–40, 397; Breese, 228–30; Robinson and Robinson, 332–34; Hunter, 266–68; Pillsbury, 326–28.

2

II. REACTION TIMES (Individual or Group)

Problem: To study, by the reaction-time method, different degrees of complexity of behavior shown in different types of situation-and-response.

Individual Method
A. The Simple Reaction

Materials: Vernier chronoscope.

Procedure: This experiment tests the time of reaction to a simple visual stimulus. The two pendulum-bobs are to be adjusted until the longer makes 75 complete swings in one minute, the shorter, 77. The wires attached to the pendulum-bobs are then slipped under the metal caps of the proper keys. S is seated in such a way as to face the key which releases the shorter pendulum, with his forefinger resting on the key. E places himself so as to face the key that releases the longer pendulum, his finger on the key. S is to react by pressing his key as soon as he sees E's key move.

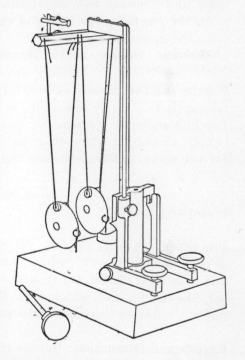

When all is ready, E says "Ready," waits between 1 and 2 seconds and presses his key. This releases the longer pendulum. As S reacts, the shorter pendulum is released. E counts the beats of the longer pendulum, calling the first back-swing "one." The counting is continued until the two pendulums come to swing in unison for a brief time. The number of beats until unison is clearly noted (do not judge too quickly!) gives the reaction in fiftieths of a second.[1] Multiply this figure by 20, and the result is in thousandths of a second, or *sigma* (σ). E is not to try to catch S unawares: if he does so, discard the reading. Repeat until 20 reactions are given. S and E then change places.

---

[1] From the data given it can readily be computed that the longer pendulum makes one complete swing in .8 seconds; the shorter in .7792 seconds. The difference between the two, .0208 seconds, may for this type of measurement be considered one fiftieth of a second.

E and S should make a number of preliminary trials before starting to record any. Occasionally S's will give abnormally short (under 100σ) or abnormally long (over 250σ) reactions; in which cases E should discard them as due to disturbing factors that should have been controlled. The student must beware of anticipatory accessory movements by E that might furnish S with a cue; too constant a fore-period between the warning and the signal; S being distracted by extraneous sights and sounds; and so forth. In these and similar cases the time may well be discarded. In general, this experiment is an excellent one for teaching the student to be on his guard against sources of error.

As the experiment goes on, S should keep in mind the following questions, and E should note any comments on them:
1. In the reaction, was S attending directly to the stimulus (E's key) or to the movement to be made?
2. Was the reaction made deliberately, or did it go off of itself?

Results and Discussion: Set down in your notes the results in the following tabular form. Prepare a table in which successive columns are labeled *Trial, Number of Swings, Sigma,* and *Comments.* In the last column (which should be wider than the others) put down any comments the subject makes. Find and note the average of the times.

B. Choice Reaction

Materials: As in *A.*

Procedure: As in *A,* with the following variations. E holds the forefinger of each hand on the key, which is to be pressed in irregular order with left and with right forefinger. S is to react with his *left* hand when E uses his *left,* likewise for the right hand. Repeat for 20 trials as before, recording but not counting incorrect responses. Then reverse positions.

Results and Discussion: Record the results as before, noting in addition whether E used his right or his left hand on each occasion, and the occurrence of any wrong response. In finding the average, throw out any wrong responses.
1. How do the times compare with those in *A?*
2. In what ways does this experiment differ from *A?*

C. Perceptual Reaction

Materials: Blank showing 100 patches of color each 1 cm. square. (The five sample patches are to be disregarded.) Watch with second hand.

4

Procedure: E lays the blank before S, showing only the five sample colors at the bottom, which S is asked to name. When this has been done, E is to start S when the second hand is at "60" by exposing the whole blank and saying "Go." S names the colors aloud, reading each line from left to right. The total time is taken. E and S then change places and the experiment is repeated, the blank this time being so placed that the sample line of colors comes at the top.

Results and Discussion: Record the total time, and, by dividing by 100, the average time for each response. Reduce to sigma.
1. How does this average compare with those in *A* and *B*?
2. How does the experiment differ from *A* and *B*?

D. Substitution Reaction

Materials: Blanks showing at the top a key of ten digits and corresponding letters; and showing below rows of digits to which correct letters are to be supplied. Watch with second hand.

Procedure: The printed sheet is to be placed *face down* until the experiment actually begins. E, with the second hand of the watch at "60," gives the signal "Go." S turns over the sheet and with his pencil proceeds to fill in under each digit the correct letter according to the code given at the top of the page. He should work as fast as possible. The total time is taken by E and recorded on the sheet. E and S then change places and repeat, using the other sheet. E should avoid looking at either sheet until he has acted as S.

Results and Discussion: Find the average time for each act of substitution. Reduce to sigma.
1. How does this compare with the times in the other parts of the whole experiment?
2. How does the situation, and how does the response, differ from that in *C*?

General

General Discussion (on whole experiment):
1. Is there a uniform increase in time required for response in the different parts *A* to *D*?
2. Is there an increase in complexity of the stimulus or situation, of the central adjustment, or of the motor response?
3. Carefully describe anything in your procedure or apparatus that might produce errors or inaccuracies in your results.

5

Group Method

Procedure: Seat the group in continuous rows to form an unbroken chain. I is to apply a stimulus to the first member, his reaction to be a stimulus to the second, and so on down the line. I is to record the total time elapsing between his applying the first stimulus and the reaction of the last individual in the chain (which may be indicated by slapping the hand on a desk, by voice, or other appropriate response).

A. The Simple Reaction

A light tap on the shoulder is used. Upon receiving a tap (stimulus) each individual "passes it on" by giving a tap (his response) to the next individual. Each individual should be turned 90° in his chair, and at I's "ready" signal should have a hand held close to the shoulder of the next person. At least five trials should be taken after at least three practice trials. I notes the total time for the group with a stop watch. The results are to be tabulated on the blackboard under the headings: *Time, Number of Individuals, Time for Average Individual, Same Reduced to Sigma.* A final average of the individual averages is computed.

B. Choice Reaction

Proceed as in *A*, with this variation: each person holds both hands near the shoulders of next person in the chain, and is to react with his *left* hand when he has just been tapped on the *right* shoulder, and vice versa.

C. Free Association Reaction

Vocal stimuli and responses are now to be used. A word spoken aloud by I serves as a stimulus to the first person in the chain, his reaction to be the quick speaking aloud of the first word which comes to his tongue upon hearing I's word. This response serves as a stimulus to the next person, and so on.

D. Judgment Reaction

As a preliminary each person silently says to himself the name of some edible thing. I speaks aloud his word. The first member of the chain *chooses* silently between the edible so named and the one he has named silently to himself, and then speaks *aloud* the name of his *preference*. This is the stimulus to the next person, and so on.

Discussion: All questions for parts *A*, *B*, *C*, *D*, and *General*, as given above.

References: Dashiell, 3–4, 45–48; Titchener, 428–50; Robinson and Robinson, 625–28; Warren and Carmichael, 292–96; Woodworth, 234–36; Gates, 83–85, 87.

6

III. ATTITUDES IN REACTION TIMES (Individual or Group)

Problem: To measure the part played by the subject's attitude or set in the quickness of his reactions.

Individual Method

Materials: Vernier chronoscope.

A. Length of Fore-Period

Procedure: The method is in general the same as that followed in the preceding experiment on "Reaction Times." S faces the key that operates the shorter pendulum (making 77 swings per sec.), E the one operating the longer (making 75). E gives a warning "Ready" and after a given interval presses his key; and S, as quickly as possible after he sees E's key pressed, is to press his own. E counts the beats of the longer pendulum until it and the shorter one are in unison. This number gives the time elapsing between stimulus and response in fiftieths of a second.

E is now to control the time-interval between his "ready" signal and his stimulus signal (key) by running the following series:

(A) 10 reactions in which this fore-period is kept absolutely constant, at 1.0 second.

(B) 10 in which this fore-period is varied in irregular order from as short as $\frac{1}{4}$ sec. to as long as 3 or 4 seconds.

(C) 10 as in series (A).

(D) 10 as in series (B).

E may follow the above order, A–B–C–D, or may follow B–A–D–C, without informing S at any time what series is being used.

Results: E keeps a careful record of the series. At the end he averages the time-intervals recorded by the A and C method and those by the B and D method.

B. The Three Types of Simple Reaction

Procedure: After a preliminary series of about 5 reactions, secure a total of 60, in this order:

(A)	5 'natural'	(B)	5 'natural'
	10 'sensorial'		10 'sensorial'
	10 'muscular'		10 'muscular'
	5 'natural'		5 'natural'

To prevent fatigue, rest after each 15, and E and S exchange places after A series and after B series (each acting as S for the total of 60).

7

For the '*Natural*' reaction: S is to keep attending to the reaction *as a whole*, not to force his attention in any particular direction but to react in a natural and 'usual' way.

For the '*Sensorial*' reaction: S is to attend especially to the sensory *stimulus*, i.e., E's key. After the warning signal has been given he is to think only of the sight of that key being pressed down, and is to keep his eye 'peeled' for that happening. He should let his own finger movement take care of itself. (To facilitate S's maintaining this sensorial attitude E may occasionally introduce a false finger movement without pressing key.)

For the '*Muscular*' reaction: S is to attend especially to *his own* movement, is to make his finger fairly 'tingle to go.' He will, of course, meanwhile keep his eye fixated on E's key, but his own finger is to be made tense and alert, all ready to go.

Note: To maintain these three distinct waiting attitudes will not be so easy for S as it may seem! He must give the task his undivided care! And the work must not be hurried!

Results: Take down readings in tabular form. Then, using cross-rule paper, on one scale draw three graphs to show the distributions of the Natural, the Sensorial, and the Muscular reaction times.

Discussion:
1. Find a concrete illustration from everyday behavior of the principle in *A*.
2. Formulate a statement of this principle in general terms.
3. Does a comparison of your averages for the different types in Procedure *B* agree with standard findings? If not, can you offer a possible explanation?
4. Offer an example of everyday behavior that resembles the Sensorial type; one that resembles the Muscular.
5. In reaction time work "what is measured is ... the time needed to set in action a previously prepared adjustment." Is this suggested or not by your results? Explain.
6. What sources of possible error are there in your procedure or in the apparatus?

Group Method

Procedure and Results: Use *B* above adapted to the group-chain method of the preceding experiment.

Discussion: Use questions 3, 4, 5, 6, above.

References: Dashiell, 43, 47–48, 277, 564–65; others as for preceding experiment.

8

IV. GROSS MUSCULAR FATIGUE (Individual or Group)

Problem: To measure the onset of muscular fatigue as affecting strength and as affecting speed.

Materials: Finger dynamometer. Bell-metronome. Tapping board and stylus. Kymograph. Double signal marker. Seconds pendulum. Batteries.

Procedure:

A. Finger Dynamometer

S's arm is laid upon the arm-board of the dynamometer, the edge of which is flush with the edge of the table. He then lays the first joints of fore and second fingers in the dynamometer stirrup, thus bringing the arm

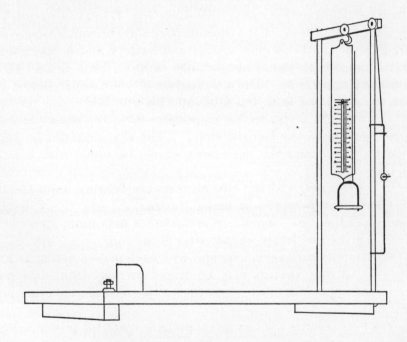

into strong (but not painful) extension at the wrist-joint. The pull is to be exerted in this position; it is to consist of an effort to pull down without using the forearm above the wrist. Practice may be necessary to overcome a tendency to strain also the muscles of the upper arm and shoulder, or to pull in some direction other than straight downward. For practice have the right arm try to maintain a maximal pull for about 20 seconds, S watching the indicator on the kilogram scale and trying to keep it low.

Repeat with the left arm. Plenty of rest should be allowed before the formal experiments. (S may rest while E is practicing.)

In the experiment proper E should read from the kilogram scale (on left) the exact position (to $\frac{1}{10}$ kg.) of the pointer every 5 seconds, and jot down the successive readings on convenient paper. The five-second intervals may be sounded for E by the proper adjustment of the metronome-with-bell so that the bell sounds every 5 seconds. The pull by S should be maintained for 60 seconds, with his attention riveted throughout on the pointer and on his pull. E will obtain 13 readings.

S and E exchange places and repeat the experiment.

Next, the left hand is used for the pull, each person acting once as S.

Each student is to report the experiment conducted by himself as E.

B. Tapping Board

See that the board and stylus (cf. Dashiell, Fig. 17) are in circuit with a signal marker and battery; that a seconds pendulum or contact-metronome is in circuit with another signal marker and battery and is operating the marker; and that both signal markers are ready to bear against smoked paper on the kymograph. (Draw a diagram of your connections.)

S is to sit with his side to the table and his arm laid along the board. He is to tap with the stylus as fast as possible upon the brass plate, from the signal "go" until the signal "stop." The elbow should be kept at rest upon the board and the movement should be made with hand and forearm only.

When S is prepared, and the two markers are bearing upon the drum with just sufficient pressure to make tracings, E sets the kymograph going and gives the "go" signal. S maintains a maximum speed of tapping, until E gives the "stop" signal after 80 seconds.

This may be done with each arm, and with each person acting as E, but alternately. All four records may be traced on one drum, one person being given the upper half of the space for his two records, the other person the lower half.

When the four records are complete, prepare them for preservation: — Carefully remove the paper from the drum without cutting the drum and without smearing yourselves with soot. Pass it through the bath of shellac-and-alcohol. Hang it up to dry.

Results and Discussion:

1. Count the number of taps made in Procedure B in each successive 3-seconds interval by inspection of the kymograph tracings.

10

2. Draw fatigue curves from your data in Procedures *A* and *B*. Compare them with the first and last curves in Figure 16 of the text, pointing out likenesses and differences.
3. What difference is there, in method of muscular contraction, between your experiment in *A* and that referred to in the text? Which method would you suppose more quickly fatiguing? Why?
4. Compare your right-hand and left-hand curves, pointing out any interesting differences.
5. Is "fatigue" the same as the "feeling of weariness"?
6. Using your best judgment, classify the following factors according to their effect upon muscular endurance into those (*A*) increasing it and those (*B*) decreasing it: a previous sleep; small dose of alcohol; large dose of alcohol; grief; moderate meal; heavy meal; high room temperature; coffee; high humidity; tobacco; band music; sad news from home; news of a varsity victory.

Method for Group

Procedure: Proceed as in *A* above. E posts his readings on the blackboard while the class copies them. If kymograph records are taken they should, when dry, be mounted under glass; and individuals of the class then or later should obtain their results by directly copying the tracings through thin paper.

Discussion: Adapt questions 2–6.

References: Dashiell, 58–59, Fig. 17; Robinson and Robinson, XXII; Pillsbury, 541–45; Watson, 182–84; Gates, 581–84; Perrin and Klein, 67; Warren and Carmichael, 44, 385.

V. TESTS OF MANUAL DEXTERITY (INDIVIDUAL OR GROUP)

Problem: In industrial psychology a great field of research is the devising of differential tests that will select the fit from the unfit applicants for a given job, including jobs that call for manual skill. Our problem is to become familiar with, and to analyze, certain well-known tests of muscular efficiency.

Materials: Hand dynamometer. Tapping board and stylus. Electric counter, key, and batteries. Coördination plate. Printed blank. (Cf. Dashiell, Fig. 17.)

Procedure:

A. Hand Dynamometer

With a millimeter rule measure the distance from where S's thumb joins his hand to the end of his fingers; adjust the dynamometer by whirling the inner stirrup until the scale on the outer stirrup indicates one half this distance, and close the clutch to prevent further turning.

S is to take a firm grip on the stirrups and is to exert a *maximal* effort, pulling as *hard* as he possibly can. E will read the amount of the grip from the dial, and record it. S is to make 3 pulls with each hand, right and left alternately, with pauses of at least 10 seconds.

The best record made with each hand is the one to be used for reference.

B. Tapping Board

See that the board and stylus are in circuit with the electric counter and battery. (Diagram your connections.) S is to sit with his side toward the table and with his arm along the board. He is to tap with the stylus as fast as possible upon the brass plate, from the signal "go" until the signal "stop." The elbow should be kept at rest upon the board and the movements should be made with hand and forearm.

When all is prepared, E gives the "go" signal and then closes his key. After exactly 20 seconds, he opens his key and then calls "stop." After a suitable rest period S repeats, using the left hand.

C. Coördination Plate

See that the metal plate (punched with holes) and stylus are in circuit with the electric counter, key, and battery. (Diagram.) Place the plate flush with the edge of the table in front of S's right shoulder, S sitting. S is to hold the stylus near the lower end of the handle, and at the signal

12

is to place and hold the needle for 15 sec. about one half inch within the largest hole without touching the sides. Hand and arm must be unsupported. E is to allow S about 2 seconds for getting the needle into position in the hole, and then is to close his key. At the end of 15 seconds, E should open the key, give the "stop" signal to S, and record the number of contacts shown on the electric counter. (The three largest holes need not be used.)

Next, test the same hole for S in a standing position and holding the stylus at arm's length. Repeat both these tests for each hole in order.

D. Tracing Test

Place a printed blank on the table before S and provide him with a fountain pen or pencil. Have the metronome beating two thirds second. Starting at point X, S is to trace the open pathway through the maze from right to left at the rate of one stroke (horizontal or vertical) to each beat of the metronome, striving not to touch any of the side lines. Upon reaching the left end of one line he is to lift the pen to the X in the next line below, being allowed 2 beats for this change.

Use one sheet for each person as S.

For results count the total number of times S made contact with or crossed a line.

Results:

1. Determine S's "index of right-handedness" (what per cent of his right-hand efficiency is his left-hand efficiency?), both with the dynamometer and with the tapping board. Does this index correspond to S's report as to whether he is right- or left-handed, and is decidedly so or only partly so, in his usual handling of things?

   Tabulate from the blackboard all the scores made by different individuals in the various tests.
2. Does an individual making a high score in one test tend to make a high score in all others? in certain ones? in which?
3. Does an individual making a low score in one test tend to make a low score in all others? in certain ones? in which?

   (This touches on the broad question of "individual differences" and their mathematical measurement — to be taken up later in course.)

Discussion:

1. Was S more efficient on the coördination plate when sitting or when standing? State your explanation in terms of muscles and joints involved in each performance.

13

2. Do the comparisons in questions under Results (2) and (3) bear out the popular assumption that "muscular ability" is a single general trait?
3. Which of the tests would best serve as an indicator of the following specific capacities:

<table>
<tr><td>a. reaction time</td><td>d. speed</td></tr>
<tr><td>b. steadiness in position</td><td>e. steadiness in</td></tr>
<tr><td>c. strength</td><td>movement</td></tr>
</table>

4. Which of the tests would you expect to be useful for selecting fitness for each of the following occupations?

    If giving more than one, underscore the most useful.   Arrange in a table.

<table>
<tr><td>a. typist</td><td>g. telegraph operator</td></tr>
<tr><td>b. engraver</td><td>h. inspector of apples</td></tr>
<tr><td>c. boiler maker</td><td>before shipping</td></tr>
<tr><td>d. steam shovel operator</td><td>i. lathe operator</td></tr>
<tr><td>e. railway mail clerk</td><td>j. surgeon</td></tr>
<tr><td>f. auto repair man</td><td></td></tr>
</table>

In each case state exactly what it is about the nature of the job that calls for ability which is tested by the test you have named.
5. Arrange all the tests in order to show on which tests the scores would probably be most affected by ill-health, which next most, etc.
6. Range the tests again to show on which tests the scores would probably be most interfered with by emotional excitability in a worker.   Is there any implication as to which of the vocations mentioned above would be poor for the nervous, excitable person to select?
7. In your opinion is it more adequate to use a single psychological test or a group of several tests in selecting applicants for a job?   Why? Defend your answer carefully.

References: Dashiell, 59–62, Fig. 17.

VI. WORK AND FATIGUE IN SEMI–IMPLICIT ACTIVITY
(INDIVIDUAL)

Problem: To measure continuous thinking work and its changes, especially changes caused by fatigue.

Materials: Tables of numbers in vertical columns for cumulative adding.

Procedure: S is to be comfortably seated in a quiet room. E is to pronounce aloud a number. S is immediately to add 2 to this number aloud, then to add 3 to this new sum, then 4 to that, then 5, and then again 2, 3, 4, 5, etc., in rotation. For instance, if the number given were 9, the consecutive sums would be: 11, 14, 18, 23, 25, 28, 32, 37, 39, etc. Every thirty seconds E is to announce a new number with which S is to start at once anew. Keep adding throughout at your *maximum speed!*

Taking first some column of numbers, E should offer S a trial by speaking aloud the number at the top, and should check his accuracy in the adding by following down the column. If a mistake is made call out the correct number and at the same time make a dot opposite it on the page.

For the formal experiments, E uses the columns in their order, from left to right. The numbers to be announced every thirty seconds to S are the ones at the tops of the columns. As S adds aloud, E follows down each column and corrects and marks errors. At the end of each thirty seconds he draws a line under the last number given by S to indicate how many numbers were added and at the same time announces aloud the new number of the next column.

One person as S is to work constantly in *one single bodily position* until he has been taken over twenty columns three times — a total of 30 minutes of adding time. He should be seated looking at a point on the wall and throughout his work he should not vary his bodily posture, but keep the same sitting position, both feet flat on the floor, head and neck and arms in the same pose, etc. This is important!

The other S is to be allowed to change his bodily postures at will while he works, arising to stand or step about, moving his hands or feet, etc., but adding continually, for the same length of time.

Results: Construct a curve in black to show the total number of additions made in each successive 30-second period (each column), and one in red, to show the number of errors. Each person should keep copies of records of both subjects, so that a comparison may be made of the two methods used.

Discussion:

1. If there are evidences of fatigue do they seem to have coincided with S's reports of "weariness" closely, loosely, or not at all? (Answer with care.) What would you theoretically expect on this?
2. Is the decrease in efficiency shown more in speed or in accuracy?
3. Is the course of implicit work and fatigue as simple and regular as that of overt work and fatigue?
4. Is there any significant difference in the work done by the two different subjects? Does this suggest what fatigue after hard study really is?
5. Arai, after multiplying four-place numbers by four-place numbers (without paper) for 12 hours uninterruptedly, showed only about 50 per cent reduction in efficiency. Is this to be expected, in light of your own results? But the office clerk or school child could not work this way: what is the difference in motivation?

References: Dashiell, 58–59, 360–62; Watson, 369–79; Robinson and Robinson, 770–89; Pillsbury, 546–47; Gates, 584–89.

VII. INTERDEPENDENCE OF THE ENDOCRINES: DRAWING
(Individual)

Procedure: Copy on drawing paper in careful detail, but on a scale of 2, Figure 21 on p. 69 of Dashiell, drawing the endocrines in heavy ink. Label stomach, kidneys, sex glands, brain parts, windpipe, and lungs (sketching more of the last named). (Somewhat similar figures that might be used for copying are to be found in Warren and Carmichael, Fig. 27, p. 50, and Perrin and Klein, Fig. 12, p. 70.)

Now, introduce into the drawing lines running from one endocrine to another, to indicate schematically facts or suppositions concerning endocrinal interrelations. Use arrowheads to indicate direction of the influence, and $+$, $-$, $\pm$, or ? to indicate its character as reënforcing, retarding or inhibiting, both, or doubtful.

Represent in this manner the many points mentioned in the examples (1) to (4) on p. 77, looking up some necessary details on the preceding pages.

Also represent the interrelations suggested by each of the following: — Eppinger, Falta and Rudinger used a triangle to show schematically: a mutual inhibition between thyroid and pancreas, a mutual inhibition between pancreas and adrenals, a mutual reënforcement between adrenals and thyroid.

After removal of the parathyroids, the thyroid often hypertrophies; and vice versa.

Atrophy of thyroid leads to enlargement of pituitary; and vice versa.

Epinephrin accelerates the production of blood-sugar by the liver.

Insulin accelerates the oxidation or using up of blood-sugar.

After removal of ovaries in female and castration in male, the pituitary is enlarged, the thyroid atrophies, the thymus persists.

Note: (*a*) Some of the interrelations mentioned consist of direct chemical or hormonic effects of gland upon gland; but (*b*) more often they are general systemic effects of one gland that play upon another simply as a part of the whole organism; and (*c*) in still other cases the interrelation is a similarity or contrast between the effects of the two glands upon other parts of the organism.

Discussion: Some of the names of glands used above really designate multiple glands.
1. Which of the names refer to organs having duct gland functions as well as the endocrine functions?

17

2. Which of the names refer to organs or regions that include at least two distinct endocrine functions? In each case point out what these distinct endocrines are.

References: Dashiell, 68–78; Watson, 197–213; Perrin and Klein, 68–71; Gates, 87–92; Warren and Carmichael, 49–52.

VIII. CUTANEOUS SENSITIVITY: TWO–POINT DISCRIMINATION (Individual)

Problem: To determine the accuracy of localization and discrimination of pressure stimulations on the skin.

Materials: Two-point esthesiometer.

Procedure: E is to place the esthesiometer upon S's forearm, with the two points parallel with the median line of the arm, sometimes touching both points to the skin and sometimes touching only one point. S, with

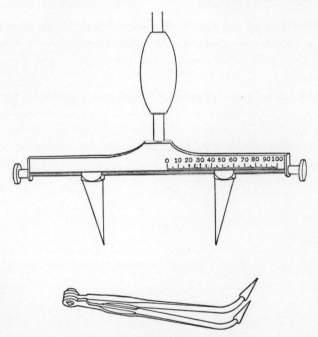

Two models of esthesiometer

eyes closed, is to respond by reporting whether one point or two are stimulating him. Several trials are to be made with the esthesiometer always turned in the same direction, and by using one point and two points for stimulation in irregular order. Start with the points widely separated and make 5–10 trials. If S reports the 2-point and 1-point stimulations correctly in 100 per cent of the trials, narrow the distance for a new set of trials. Continue in this manner until a setting of the esthesiometer is reached at which S makes about 80 per cent correct judgments (the "threshold"). Try also a few shorter distances to make certain of your threshold. Now, starting with the two points together, gradually widen the distance between them, using 1-point and 2-point stimulations in irregular order, until an 80 per cent threshold is found.

Repeat the procedure, this time turning the esthesiometer so that it lies *at right angles* to the median line of the arm.

Another area (forehead, cheek, or back of neck; also finger tip or lip) is to be measured in the same way.

Results: For each area, and each direction, average the two thresholds found.

Discussion:
1. In which direction on the arm is the accuracy of discrimination greater?
2. Do you find differences between the different areas in discrimination? Can such differences be of practical importance to the living organism? Consider carefully.
3. Which of the three main psychophysical methods does your procedure illustrate?

References: Dashiell, 87–88, 116–17; Hunter, 265–66; Robinson and Robinson, 309–11; Warren and Carmichael, 148–50.

IX. OLFACTORY SENSITIVITY: EXHAUSTION (Individual)

Problem: To study the rate of smell adaptation or exhaustion, and the selectivity of odors by this method.

Materials: Bottles of various odorous substances. Cotton. Watch.

A. Progressive Exhaustion

Procedure and Results:

Let S thoroughly stop one nostril with cotton or otherwise. Then S or E should hold one of the bottles to the open nostril until it can no longer be smelled. Time the period in which it can be smelled. Rest at least 1 minute and repeat. Make 10 trials; and average the results. Repeat the above, using another odor.

Caution: Do not place corks in wrong bottles!!

B. Selectivity of Exhaustion

Let S familiarize himself with the smells of oil of cloves and of creosote in separate bottles. Take the bottle with a mixture of the two. Is the odor of each to be detected or of only one? Now exhaust the nostril for the *pure* creosote in the original bottle. This done, let him smell again the *mixed* solution. What can be detected this time?

Discussion:
1. What relation obtains between the number of exhaustion periods and the exhaustion time?
2. What do your results indicate in regard to the simplicity of the olfactory end organ?
3. Describe a situation in everyday life in which the principle of olfactory exhaustion is exemplified.
4. How could you revise the procedure of this experiment to make it a strictly objective one — not relying at all upon any verbal reporting by your S? Could it be performed on a lower animal?

References: Dashiell, 92; Titchener, 124–25; Breese, 134; Gates, 147–48.

X. AUDITORY SENSITIVITY: SOME TONAL INTERRELATIONS
(GROUP)

Problem: To analyze some of the interrelations of sounds.

Materials: Sonometer (wire string stretched over sounding board). Two identical tuning forks, one variable. Quincke's tubes.

Procedure and Results:

A. Timbre

Tune the wire of the sonometer in perfect unison with a tuning fork; then sound them together.

1. What is the difference in the two sounds, and to what physical difference is it due?

This is to be demonstrated further. I plucks the wire string, and as the tone is sounding touches it lightly with cotton wad, brush, or finger, at the halfway point. What is heard? Compare with the original sound of the undamped string. Repeat by damping at one quarter and one third distance on string.

2. What is the relationship of overtone to fundamental in each of the three cases stated (a) in musical terminology (minor third, fifth, major seventh, octaves, etc.), and (b) in terms of mathematical relationships of the physical vibration rates?

B. Beats

I sounds simultaneously two tuning forks that are of identical pitch (one a standard fork of known vibration rate, the other a fork made variable by sliding weight or by additions of wax). Beats are heard. I changes the tone of the variable fork through a considerable range; and with each change the S's are to count the number of beats produced within a 10-sec. period marked off by visual signals given by I. Repeat each 2 or more times, and find the average per second. When the beats are fast, counting can best be done in twos, as "One-ty, two-ty, three-ty," etc.

1. For each setting of the variable fork arranged by I, list all beat counts made and the average.
2. With the vibration rate of the standard fork known, state the vibration frequencies of the variable fork for each setting.
3. With a sketch of wave forms explain graphically how beats occur.

C. Combination Tones

I sounds together two Quincke tubes, and members of the group listen attentively to detect the presence of a third tone not produced at all when either tube is sounded alone.

1. Is the new tone higher or lower than either or both of the original tones?
2. Describe any difference between this combination tone and the generating tones, as to intensity, localization, beats, etc.
3. Which of the various combination tones is this one?

Discussion: Are the phenomena studied in this experiment primarily psychological or physical in their explanation or interpretation? Answer carefully.

References: Dashiell, 102–04; Titchener, 100–09; Breese, 156–61; Warren and Carmichael, 114–16; Hunter, 246–49; Robinson and Robinson, 243–47.

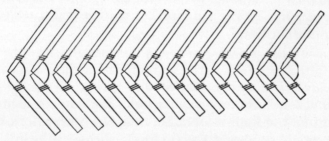

Sonometer and Quincke's tubes

XI. VISUAL SENSITIVITY: COLOR MIXING (INDIVIDUAL OR GROUP)

Problem: To demonstrate the laws of color mixture.

Materials: Color wheel. Colored disks. Smaller disks of black and white. Protractor. (Cf. Dashiell text, Fig. 34, p. 111.)

Procedure and Results:

A. (Individual method.) E places on the mixer disks of blue and yellow. Begin with 180 degrees of each color, and vary the amount of color until the colors cancel, giving gray. Keeping this proportion constant, place on the mixer the smaller white and black disks, and revolve these together with the blue and yellow, varying the proportion of black and white until S reports that the grays match. If the outer disks now are seen to have some color, vary them until they match some proportion of the inner disks. (Make sure!) Measure the amount of each disk exposed in degrees.

Repeat for red and green. (On account of the impurity of colors provided, a third may be required here. Which?)

Express results in form of an equation, thus:

$$162° \text{ yellow} + 198° \text{ blue} = 187° \text{ white} + 173° \text{ black.}$$

(Group method.) For the group proceed as above except that I acts as E and all members of the class serve as S's. I is to arrive at each final determination of a color ratio according to majority judgments of the group, this ratio then being ascertained numerically from the rotator and announced to the members of the group for their individual recording.[1]

B. (Individual and group methods are here identical.) E or I is to mix red and yellow; mix yellow and green; mix green and blue. Each S is to describe the resultant colors, and state how they vary as the relative amount of exposed surface of the two disks varies. Where double names are used to identify a color (as, bluish-green), use a noun for the predominate color, an adjective for the other color.

Note the arrangement of the colors in the color spectrum. Where do the colors produced by each mixture lie with regard to the two colors from which it was produced?

C. (Individual and group methods as in *A.*) Place together on the color wheel both mixtures used in *A*, the blue-yellow and the red-green,

---

[1] A differential color wheel when graduated and scaled makes possible individual reactions by the class members, eliminating the cruder majority-judgment method. I, when nearing the threshold, can change the ratio degree by degree, announcing each, and the individual S can note down the ratio announced when he individually reacts to the mixture as to gray.

but use 180 degrees of each of the two mixtures above, the colors being in the same proportions.   What results?

Discussion:
1. From the results of your experiment verify the Laws of Color Mixture: (*A*) for Complementary colors, (*B*) for Non-complementary colors, and (*C*) for Combinations of colors.   Are any revisions of these laws suggested by your results?
2. Just why do colors mix or fuse on a rotating disk?
3. State other examples of the principle here involved.
4. Distinguish this principle from that involved in the mixture of pigments.
5. Why is it difficult to name correctly the colors of fabrics seen under ordinary artificial light?

References: Dashiell, 110–11; Breese, 184; Titchener, 67–70; Robinson and Robinson, 216–18; Pillsbury, 111–12; Gates, 154–56; Hunter, 255–56.

XII. VISUAL SENSITIVITY: RETINAL COLOR ZONES
(INDIVIDUAL OR GROUP)

Problem: To determine the different areas of retinal sensitivity to colors.

Materials: Perimeter with hand rod and five color squares. (Cf. Dashiell text, Fig. 35, p. 113.)

Procedure: Perimeter is clamped upright. S closes one eye and with the open eye looks over the eye-guide in such a way that the pupil is fixated by its own reflection in the mirror. E attaches the Red color square to the hand rod and holds it against the inner side of the arc and a little to the right of the mirror, so that S can identify it. Then E slowly moves the color outward along the arc toward the periphery at the right. S, *keeping his eye steadily fixated* in the mirror, attends to the moving color and reports "there" at the moment it disappears *as red*, i.e., changes to gray or some other color. E records the point of disappearance in degrees read from the back of the arc. E now reverses the procedure, starting the color from near the periphery (90° on arc) and moving it toward the center until S reports "there" at its reappearance *as red*. Repeat both "in" and "out" procedures until close agreement in the two reports is obtained.

Determine similarly the point of appearance-disappearance for each of the other three colors and the gray.

Repeat the procedure for the four colors and gray for distances to the LEFT of the fixation point; also (by turning the arc vertically) for distances ABOVE and BELOW. E will then have a graph of 40 readings.

Results: Take down readings in tabular form, as:

COLOR.........red..............

Trial	Nasal		Temporal		Superior		Inferior	
	In	Out	In	Out	In	Out	In	Out
1	55	48	..	..	..	..	..	..
2	52	47	..					
3	..	..						
4								
5								
Totals	...	...	...	...	...	...	...	...
Grand totals		...		...		...		...
Averages		...		...		...		...

On paper MAP the visual field by marking with a dot the average of "in" and "out" readings of each color on each meridian, then connecting the four points for each color with a heavy line of that color.

Discussion:
1. Can it be said that the normal person's eye is to some degree color blind?
2. Is one aware of the existence of these color zones in everyday life? Explain why.
3. Your map is a map of the visual field. State how you would reverse it in such a way as to make a map of the retina itself.
4. Does the arrangement of these zones seem consistent with the Hering theory?
5. Is the change from gray to color sudden or gradual?
6. Where on your map would an orange be seen as such? A purple?
7. If your S were red-green color blind, how would your map be changed?

References: Dashiell, 112–13; Breese, 188–89; Titchener, 80–83; Robinson and Robinson, 222–24; Pillsbury, 116–17; Hunter, 256, 259–61; Warren and Carmichael, 95, 100–01.

XIII. KINESTHETIC SENSITIVITY AND WEBER'S LAW
(INDIVIDUAL)

Problem: To demonstrate Weber's law for kinesthetic sensitivity by the lifted weights procedure.

"This may be regarded as the classical experiment of quantitative psychology" (Titchener). It is an excellent one for training purposes as well as for the factual results: especially for directing attention to the errors creeping into experimental investigations.

A. By the Method of Limits

Materials: Empty cylinder cases. Shot. Balance scales.

Procedure: E presents a pair of weights to S, under or behind a screen, by placing first one then the other on a certain padded spot just under S's hand. Each time S is to lower his hand, take the weight between thumb and first finger and "heft" it once. After the second of each pair is hefted he should report whether it was "heavier" or "lighter" than the first (judgments of "equal" not permitted). S must lift the two weights always at the same rate and to the same height, using a forearm movement with elbow on table.

E's two weights consist of a *Standard* (of constant weight) and a *Comparison* (varying above the standard). He should begin with a Standard of low weight and a Comparison distinctly higher; making 10 presentations of the two in varying orders. (Why?) If S reports correctly for all pairs reduce the Comparison weight by taking out one or two shot; and continue this until a Comparison is found in which S can judge correctly in just 75 per cent of the trials. (Many more than 10 presentations will be necessary when the difference between Standard and Comparison approaches this point.) When the 75 per cent threshold has been found, carefully weigh the Comparison weight (also checking the Standard). Record both weights.

Repeat, using a Standard of a higher weight, and a higher Comparison. If time permits, use also a Standard of still higher weight.

B. By the Method of Constant Stimuli

Materials: Two sets of known weights of identical appearance, each set consisting of one Standard and several Comparison weights.

Procedure: Proceed as above, except that instead of changing the Comparison weight by taking out shot, substitute other Comparisons. Also,

28

S is now to be given 20 or more trials on each pair of weights in one set, in 20 series of 1 trial to each. Within each series, the order of the pairs should be varied; and within each pair, the order of S and C in different series (each being presented first a total of 10 times).

E's schedule of presentations must be made out with care. Consider the following:

1st series	2d series	3d series	.....	20th series
$S-C_1$	$S-C_2$	C_3-S		
C_3-S	C_4-S	$S-C_1$		
C_2-S	C_1-S	$S-C_4$		
$S-C_4$	$S-C_3$	C_2-S		

Treatment of data: For each weight pair total the number of correct judgments. It is unlikely that any particular weight used will yield the 75 per cent correct judgments necessary to indicate the threshold. Some will yield higher and others lower percentages, hence resort must be had to some method of interpolation. But the precise mathematical methods in use are too complicated for use here, and simpler methods are suggested.

(1) Simplified mathematical method: Suppose the threshold to lie somewhere between weight X, which has been correctly differentiated from the Standard in 88 per cent of trials, and weight Y, correctly judged in 56 per cent. Then the formula would read

$$\frac{X(75-56)+Y(88-75)}{88-56} = C \text{ at the threshold difference}$$

Apply the formula to your own data.

(2) Graphic method: On a horizontal base line represent at proper distances (abscissas) the different C weights used, and on a vertical line (ordinates) indicate percentages from 0 to 100. Then enter points on the graph to show the scores obtained for each weight pair; join these points with a heavy line; extend a dotted line from the 75 per cent level horizontally across to intersect the heavy line; from this intersection drop a dotted line vertically to the base line; and write in the weight to be interpolated there. Separate graphs will be required for the two sets of weights. They should be drawn on a large scale.

Results and Discussion (A or B):

1. For each S weight used, state the difference threshold (DL) as an absolute difference $(C-S)$; then as a relative difference $\frac{(C-S)}{S}$.

2. Do the results approximate Weber's law?

29

3. Describe any sources of error you may be able to identify in your technique: time errors, space errors, adaptation, expectation, absolute impression, fatigue, distraction, practice, etc.
4. Which of your methods is also called the Method of Just Noticeable Differences; of Right and Wrong Cases; of Minimal Changes?
5. Can you think how the lifted weights experiment might be reorganized to illustrate the Method of Average Error?
6. What other modality of sensitivity is directly affected in the "hefting"? Is the DL in this modality as low as for kinesthetic?
7. In "touch typewriting" is it really touch (cutaneous) that is trained?
8. Why should a weight to be lifted be placed on a light pad?

References: Dashiell, 93–95, 115–17; Titchener, 160–72, 215–24; Pillsbury, 181–83, 193–98; Warren and Carmichael, 134–37, 145–48; Breese, 101–03, 112–14.

XIV. CENTRAL FUNCTIONS IN THE NERVOUS SYSTEM: DRAWING (INDIVIDUAL)

Problem: To locate some simple and complex connection-functions in the central nervous system.

Materials: Figures in text. Drawing paper.

Procedure:

A. Reproductions

Copy on drawing paper, in careful detail on a scale of 2, the following figures in the Dashiell text, labeling all parts shown there.

Figure 37, p. 123. Figure 43, p. 140. Figure 41, facing p. 132. Figure 44, p. 141. (Somewhat similar figures in other texts that may be substituted are: Breese, 20, 21, 22, 30; Woodworth, 70, 74, 76, 77, 78; Pillsbury, 18, 26, 32; Warren and Carmichael, 13, 18, 20, 21; Hunter, 28, 33, 34, 37.)

B. Problems

Make a large outline drawing of cord and brain; then draw in the probable neural pathways involved in each of the following examples of behavior. Add the necessary receptors and effectors.

I. *A person after hefting a weight says "fifteen pounds."* Show by lines and arrowheads the neural pathways from the receptors stimulated by the weight to the higher centers and out to the effectors involved in the speech. Use two different colors or kinds of lines.

II. *A person is trying out a new auto horn.* (a) Show by lines and arrowheads the pathways from the receptors for sight, hearing, and touch, to their correct projection areas on the cerebral cortex; then (b) draw further lines to show how all three sensory functions are integrated in a sensory association area; (c) draw lines to show that these combined neural impulses are carried over to a motor association area; (d) draw lines to show that they are further transmitted to various motor projection centers; and finally (e) use lines to show their transmission out to the various effectors moving the arm. Use different colors or kinds of lines for (a), (b), (c), (d).

References: Dashiell, 123–42; Breese, 37, 40–52; Woodworth, 521–39; Pillsbury, 46–77; Warren and Carmichael, 27–45; Hunter, 156–73.

XV. DISSECTION OF THE BRAIN (Individual)

Problem: To identify the principal parts of the brain in their inter-relations.

Materials: Plaster of Paris models of human brain or actual specimens of animal brain. Preserved specimen of human brain (for reference). Wall plaque. Printed illustrations. Drawing paper and pencils.

Procedure and Results: (The student should familiarize himself with Figures 39, 41, 42, 43, 44, and 45 in the Dashiell textbook — or equivalent figures in other texts.)

The main work is to be done on the human model or on the animal specimen provided the student, help being available in the form of illustrations and human specimens. Since the model is fragile, it must be handled with care, and all parts except the head base must be laid upon soft cloth. The natural specimens should be laid on cotton and blotting or towel paper. MAKE NO MARKS ON MODELS, NOR ON ILLUSTRATIONS!

A. (To be omitted if animal brain is used.)

Carefully remove the whole brain from the cranium (do not drop any of the four parts). Note irregularities in the floor of the cranium: bony protuberances (right side) containing cavities holding the eye and ear apparatus (shown on the left side); hole in base through which the spinal cord leads to the brain; holes (right) through which various cranial nerves pass out (left). What is 1, and what is 12? What do you take to be the functions of 2, 5, 6, 7, 8, 11?

B. *Lateral View.* (If animal brain be used, omit references to cranium, eyes, etc.)

Replace the brain in the cranium and note its position in the head. The top of the bony skull has been removed as well as several membranes encasing the brain. Lifting the whole brain a little way out of the cranium, note the position of the brain with reference to eyes and ears and back of head. Note that the whole brain is superficially divisible in *medulla*, and *pons* (shown in white), *cerebellum* (brownish-gray), and *cerebrum* (pinkish-gray).

Draw about half-size a LATERAL full view outline of the head with the skull complete down to the bottom of the ear and nose (all this in dotted lines), and indicate the positions of the following parts in continuous lines.

(Number the parts as below and include a key to the numbers on the same page with your drawing.)

1. Frontal Lobe; 2. Temporal Lobe; 3. Parietal Lobe; 4. Occipital Lobe; 5. Fissure of Rolando (Central Fissure); 6. Post-Central Convolution (Cutaneous-Kinesthetic Area); 7. Pre-Central Convolution (Motor Area); 8. Fissure of Sylvius (Lateral Fissure); 9. Pons; 10. Cerebellum; 11. Cranial Nerves; 12. Medulla; 13. Spinal Cord.

C. Median View

Carefully part the brain along the median line into right and left halves. (Consult human specimens, and Dashiell text, Fig. 41.) Note how the medulla, rising from the spinal cord, is thickened at the place where the pons forms a horizontal band of fibers running around the medulla into the cerebellum. Note the configuration of white matter in the cross-section of the cerebellum, the *arbor vitæ*. Next above the cerebellum are found four little protuberances, the *corpora quadrigemina* (not always well shown on the model), two on each side of the median line. Still higher are found the right and left halves of the *thalamus*, a rounded mass at about the center of the whole brain. (The thalami are more completely separated in some animals than in man.) A little higher is seen a long curved band (shown in white) composed of nerve fiber connecting the right and left halves of the cerebrum and appearing here in cross-section, the *corpus callosum*. Finally, the cerebral hemispheres themselves are the highest and most conspicuous part, having enlarged enormously and now overlying nearly all the other brain parts.

The spinal cord is essentially a tube with a greatly thickened wall. The brain is formed from the cord, and we can trace the "bore" of the tube through the *fourth ventricle, aqueduct of Sylvius, third ventricle*, and the paired *lateral ventricles* lying one in each cerebral hemisphere.

Make a good sized drawing of this median view of the brain showing and labeling the following parts:

1. Medulla; 2. Pons; 3. Pituitary Gland; 4. Optic Chiasm; 5. Corpus Callosum; 6. Third Ventricle; 7. Thalamus; 8. Aqueduct of Sylvius; 9. Corpora Quadrigemina; 10. Arbor Vitæ; 11. Fourth Ventricle; 12. Frontal Lobe; 13. Parietal Lobe; 14. Occipital Lobe; 15. Temporal Lobe; 16. Cerebellum.

D. Horizontal Cross-Section View

In all parts of the brain are found cell bodies and also their axons and dendrites. The cell bodies are in general collected in the *cortex* of the cerebellum and cerebrum (grayish portions), and also in little groups called *nuclei* scattered through the brain stem. The difference between cortex and white matter in cerebellum has been noted above.

Lift off an upper section of the right cerebral hemisphere and note the cortex forming the outside with the white matter inside. (Consult human specimen.) Draw this view about half-size, showing and labeling the following parts:

1. Gray Matter of Cortex; 2. White Matter; 3. Convolutions; 4. Sulci (furrows); 5. Island of Reil.

Discussion:

1. Briefly give the functions or other significance of each of the following parts in the same order as given below: (1) Occipital Lobe; (2) Fissure of Rolando; (3) Fissure of Sylvius; (4) Post-Central Convolution; (5) Pre-Central Convolution; (6) Pons; (7) Cerebellum; (8) Cranial Nerves; (9) Medulla; (10) Spinal Cord; (11) Optic Nerve; (12) Optic Chiasm; (13) Olfactory Bulb and Stalk; (14) Pituitary Gland; (15) Longitudinal Fissure; (16) Corpus Callosum; (17) Ventricles; (18) Thalamus; (19) Aqueduct of Sylvius; (20) Corpora Quadrigemina; (21) Arbor Vitæ; (22) Convolutions; (23) Sulci.
2. What is the difference between gray and white matter in structural detail?
3. Is it correct to speak of the brain as the elaborated end of the spinal cord? Are there any nervous functions peculiar to the brain alone?
4. "Different regions of the cerebrum have different specific and distinct functions to perform in the organism's behavior." Is such an assertion true — wholly, only partly, or not at all? Briefly summarize the correct position to take on this question.
5. Which conception of the brain seems more natural when you are actually looking at it — as a place where ideas are stored, or a place where elaborate connections are made between receptors and effectors?

References: Dashiell, 132–46; Watson, Figs. 30–35; Breese, Figs. 6–9, 19, 28–30; Warren and Carmichael, Figs. 14–18.

XVI. REFLEX ACTION (Individual or Group)

Problem (A): To identify the pupillary reflex.

Materials: Small black cardboard screen. Millimeter scale. Electric light or bright window.

Procedure and Results: S is to be seated where the illumination of his eye can be quickly increased or decreased by E's moving the black cardboard back and forth in front of, and away from, his eye. S fixates a definite point, and E observes his eyes.

1. Alternately increase and decrease the light a few times. What reaction is made at S's pupil? Have S hold a millimeter scale in front of and across his eye just below the pupil and estimate as accurately as you can the diameter of the pupil under maximum and minimum illumination.

2. Next, throw the light into one eye only, screening the other, and observe the reaction of the unscreened eye. Do you get a coördinated reflex?

Discussion:
1. What sort of connection do you suppose exists between the two eyes which makes the coördinated reflex possible?
2. Could S directly report the pupillary reflex reactions he was making? Compare with the wink and the knee-jerk reflexes in this regard.
3. Do you suppose S could have developed control over this reflex as in the case of winking? Why?

Problem (B): Is the knee-jerk reflex subject to reënforcement?

Materials: Table. Soft hammer adjusted to drop with a constant force against one place on the knee. Electric bell or other sound producer. Hand dynamometer.

Procedure: S is blindfolded and is seated on the edge of a table so that his leg below the knee hangs freely. The hammer is adjusted to strike the patellar tendon just below the knee-cap (exact point to be determined by hand taps). S is to leave his leg in a relaxed position, and is also not to change his general body position. (a) Raising the hammer to a constant height drop it against the knee and observe the amount of reflex. Repeat several times. (b) A small fraction of a second before the tap stimulus, apply a strong auditory stimulus, such as an electric bell, or a cutaneous stimulus, such as an induction needle. Observe whether the response is reënforced (facilitated). Repeat a few times, with one or more regular taps-without-sound between each two taps-with-sound. (c) Follow the same procedure, but with gripping of a hand dynamometer or of the two hands by S instead of the bell or needle stimulus. Is reënforcement present?

Results: Present a table showing the nature of the stimulation used each time and whether the kick is normal, reënforced, or inhibited.

Discussion:
1. Discuss the importance of controlling the time-interval between the incidental stimulus and the tap.
2. Describe some concrete life situation in which one seeks to increase the effect of one stimulus by presenting others of different modality; e.g., speeding up a horse or an athlete.

Problem (C): Is a reflex, such as winking, subject to wider control (influences)?

Materials: Winking glass, consisting of thick glass window with felt hammer.

Procedure: Before starting the experiment operate the hammer a few times to see how it works. It should swing down sharply to the glass. When ready for the experiment have S seated so that he can be comfortable while his head is fixed stationary before the glass and almost touching it. E then releases the hammer, letting it hit the glass directly in front of S's eyes. Does S wink? Repeat 100 times, S attempting not to wink, and record for each trial the appearance of wink, of partial wink, or of complete control. After 2 or 3 minutes' rest repeat the tests, S now holding one eye closed and trying to control the open eye.

Attach a sounder to the glass that will produce a noise when the hammer strikes, and repeat the stimulation to both eyes 50 times. Note whether the winking reaction is equal, greater, or less than without the use of the sounder.

E and S change places and repeat the experiment.

Results: Take down your results in tabular form in this manner:

	BOTH EYES		ONE EYE
1	w (wink)	1	w
2	w	2	
3	w	3	
4	pw (partial wink)	4	
5	w		
100	c (control)		(etc.)

Discussion:

1. Is there any development of a wider control of the winking function than by the visual stimulus from the hammer? Is this development rapid or slow? Is it developed consistently, with no relapses?
2. Was control secured best by any particular devices; e.g., rigid opposing muscles, gazing at an object in the distance, speaking to one's self, etc.?
3. What evidence do your results give of more or less coördination in the reflexes of the two eyes?

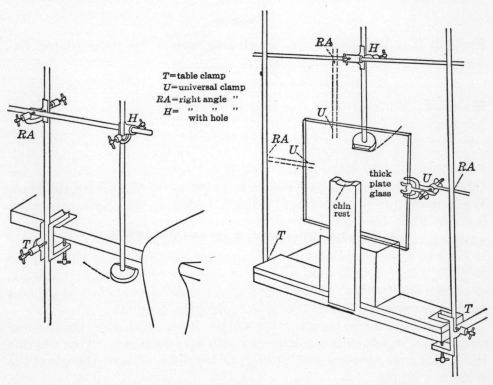

T = table clamp
U = universal clamp
RA = right angle "
H = "   "   "
    with hole

thick plate glass

chin rest

An arrangement of hammer for the knee-jerk   Winking glass

37

4. Scrutinize your technique to see whether there may be involved any facilitation or inhibition of reflexes.

5. Taking a simple reflex of class D in table, page 155 of Dashiell text (e.g., sucking, grasping, or some simple vocal sound), show descriptively how it usually becomes so greatly modified in the individual's development by being combined and re-combined into patterns of behavior that it almost loses its identity as an isolable reflex.

References: Dashiell, 155–58, 175; Warren and Carmichael, 256–64, 395–96; Robinson and Robinson, 111–18; Hunter, 175–81; Woodworth, 230–32; Perrin and Klein, 76–78.

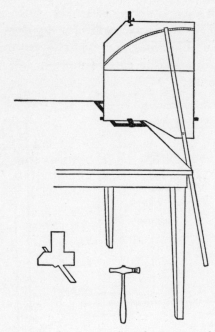

An arrangement for measuring the extent of knee-jerk

XVII. THE CONDITIONED REFLEX (GROUP)

Problem: To demonstrate the establishment of a conditioned reflex.

Materials: Kymograph. Signal markers. Electric bell. Miniature lamp. Double-contact key. Inductorium. Tambours (or relay). Batteries. Rheostat. Suitable electrodes. (Student to diagram the arrangement of apparatus that is actually used.)

Procedure: Set up the apparatus as follows. (See diagram.) The hand board is equipped with electrodes and tambour somewhat as shown in

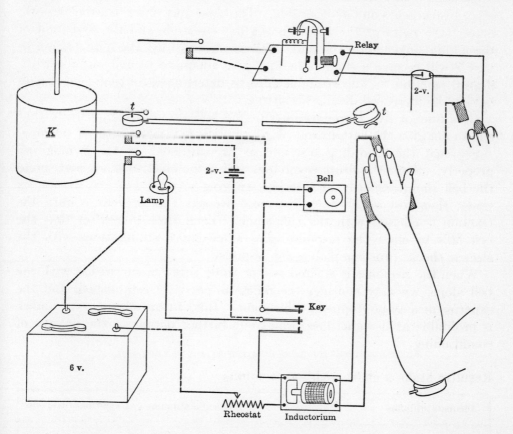

Dashiell's textbook, Figure 52, or Watson's, Figure 2. To the binding posts, which are wired under the board to the electrodes, attach leads from the secondary of an inductorium. Place the inductorium in (primary) circuit with a 6-volt battery, a rheostat, a lamp, a signal marker bearing on the kymograph drum, and the lower contacts of E's key. Place a bell

39

in series circuit with a 2-volt battery, another signal marker, and the upper contacts of the key. Connect a receiving tambour at S's finger by a tube to a recording tambour at the kymograph. When E's key is pressed lightly to bring the upper contacts together, the bell rings, and a record is made in the second line of the kymograph tracing; but when the key is pressed heavily to bring the lower contacts together, the shock is given also, the lamp is lighted as a signal to the observers, and a record is made in the third kymograph line. The smoked drum will then show: (1) a line traced pneumatically showing finger reactions, (2) a line showing incidence of the bell stimulus, (3) a line showing incidence of the shock stimulus.

S's hand board and the bell should be on one side of a screen, E and all other instruments on the other side. The class may observe latter or both. S rests the palm of the hand on the flat electrode and the first joint of the middle finger upon the narrow electrode. Adjust the inductorium so that S will receive a slight stimulus, just adequate to call out the withdrawal reaction. (This stimulus must be determined for each S, and may have to be increased during his sitting.)

Give four or five stimulations with the bell alone to demonstrate that S does not give the withdrawal reaction to the bell alone without training.

See that the recording instruments are adjusted on the kymograph properly. Start the drum revolving. Give the electric shock and sound the bell simultaneously at intervals varying around 2–3 sec. five or six times, then test with the bell alone. Repeat this procedure until the reaction is elicited with the bell alone. Each time thereafter that the bell fails to elicit the response, give a few more stimulations with the electric shock, thus compelling the response.

When the response is elicited two or three times in succession with the bell alone, we may consider the reflex as partially established, and the experiment may be stopped at this point. But, if time allows, continuance is profitable as it sometimes brings out further details of the process of conditioning.

Results: Make a chart with four columns:

Adequate stimulus	Unconditioned response	Incidental stimulus	Conditioned response

When the adequate stimulus (shock) is given as well as the bell, the student should check in the first and second columns.

When the bell is rung without the electric shock, he should check in the third column; and if there is a reaction, check in the fourth column.

Note: The student may find it impossible to take down a record during the experiment: he should make it out later by inspection of the kymograph record preserved and placed under glass by the instructor.

Discussion:
1. State essentials of the distinction between the original, adequate, or unconditioned stimulus and the incidental, inadequate, or conditioned stimulus.
2. Have you any evidence for either of the following: (*a*) irregular appearance, and (*b*) wearing out ("experimental extinction") of the c.r.?
3. Is the conditioned reflex a true reflex? Give reasons.
4. What is meant by the expression "latent time of the reflex"?
5. What is meant by the terms: specificity of the c.r.; irradiation of c.r.; and delayed c.r.?
6. In what different temporal relationships may stimuli be given in the training series to form conditioned reflexes?

References: Dashiell, 170–77; Watson, 28–38; Perrin and Klein, 92–119; Warren and Carmichael, 176–81; Hunter, 47–50; Woodworth, 151–61; Gates, 282–92.

XVIII. NATIVE PATTERNED REACTIONS IN ANIMALS
(INDIVIDUAL OR GROUP)

Problem: To identify by controlled observations, certain tendencies to patterned reactions common to a species.

Materials: White rats, as subjects. Wire screens. Large pan of water. Choice chambers with open and enclosed spaces.

Procedure and Results: Rule several sheets of note-paper in two columns, one about 3 inches wide headed SITUATION, the other about 5 inches wide headed RESPONSE. E or I is to apply various stimuli to the animals and E is to observe carefully and accurately their responses. In recording describe in each case the S (situation) and the R (response); also any variations in R produced by variations in S.

1. Place the animal on a square of wire screen and incline the screen toward the vertical. What R? Repeat, inclining the different sides in irregular order. Record R's. What receptors and what effectors are probably most involved? Can you make any general interpretations of this behavior?

2. Place the animal on the screen. Then, taking hold of the animal only, lift it bodily into the air. Does it *grasp* the screen? What human behavior does this R resemble?

3. (*a*) Observe the *righting* reaction on a table surface by laying the animal on its back and seeing whether it turns over. Describe carefully. (*b*) Hold the animal in the air 10 or 15 inches above the table (by tail, by feet, by body with back downward, etc.), and drop it. How does it land? Repeat several times with different holds and try to determine just when and how the component reflexes of the whole righting reaction occur.

4. Make a high-pitched *noise* near several animals (in nest?) by crumpling newspaper, blowing through lips, hissing, etc. Is there any characteristic R? Does this total behavior appear to have any emotional elements in it? If so, what? Try several times and be critical of your answer.

5. Hold an animal lightly in the hands in such a manner as to expose only the head. Are any constant *exploratory* movements evident? What relation is there between these and the grosser random movements of the body when the animal is free on the table? Try the latter.

6. Hold animals in the hands in close *restraint* over all of the body and limbs. Again restrain them by holding only the hindquarters, only the tail, only the forequarters, only the head. Are there any apparent inconsistencies here? Record the results for each.

7. Place an animal in water. Is any *swimming* behavior observable? Describe the movements of all four limbs, head, etc. Compare these with its movements when walking. Place an animal on a table with water on the surface, and by gentle urging give it an opportunity to enter the water. Does it seek the water?

8. (a) Taking one animal at a time, introduce it into the alley leading to the wide opening. When reaching the opening does it venture across the open space or hug one of the walls?

(b) Introduce the animal into an alley leading to a choice between covered and uncovered alleys. Which does it choose?

These trials should be repeated with the same or different animals.

Discussion:

1. A student once found that he could teach white rats always to take the upward-inclined turn at every division of pathways. Do you suppose it would have been as easy to teach them always to take the downward-inclined turn? Why?

2. Is the righting response common to many animals (including humans)? Name some of those you can think of, and describe any differences in the exact manner in which the response is made.

3. Ditto for R to sounds.

4. Ditto for swimming R.

5. Ditto for R to restraint.

6. Ditto for R to enclosures.

7. Did you judge some of the behavior to be emo-

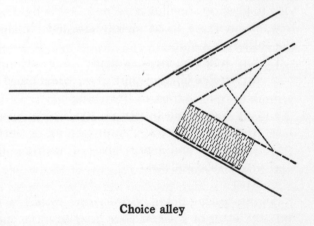

Choice alley

tional (internal, visceral) as well as instinctive (external, overt)? Can you be absolutely sure of the presence of the emotional changes by mere eye-observations? Compare the reliability or unreliability of always judging emotional changes by outward signs in the human.

References: Dashiell, 186–92, 193–96; Robinson and Robinson, 97–105; Hunter, 182–89; Woodworth, 204–14.

43

XIX. REFLEX PATTERNED REACTIONS IN CHILDREN (Group)

Problem: To identify some reflex actions as parts of a total response to odor.

Materials: Several bottles of odorous substances.

Procedure: Arrange to have one or two children serve as S's. (The children should be young enough to react naïvely and naturally, and should not be made self-conscious by the observers. Several should be tried, to increase the chances of finding a good case. Adults seldom make good S's, but can be tried, as an individual experiment, after being well cautioned to be natural and to act naturally throughout "just as if no one were watching.")

The odors are to be used in an irregular order unknown to S. S is to keep eyes closed, and I is to hold one of the bottles just under S's nose for about 10 seconds. S's attention should be directed to the *quality* of the *odor* by such questions as, "Can you tell what this is?" He should be told to keep on smelling it as long as it is held under his nose. His reactions to each odor are to be closely studied by the students with reference to the following points:

1. Any reflex changes in depth of breathing?
2. Any reflex changes in rate of breathing?
3. Any reflex arrest of breathing?
4. Any facial reflexes (brow, eyebrows, nose, mouth, etc.)?
5. Any head reflexes of approaching or withdrawing?
6. Any hand and arm reflexes of approaching or withdrawing?
7. Any vocal reflexes?
   Etc.

An interesting detail of procedure would be for I to announce each odor only by letter of a secret code, and to have the observers try to classify or to name each according to S's reactions to it. The use of several S's or of repeated trials on one S would increase the value of this part of the demonstration.

Results: Make a table showing the name of the odor in the first column and the seven or more points listed above in the other columns.

1. Make general statements based upon a comparison of the different reactions to the different kinds of odors. Did or would the reactions help you to classify the odors?

44

2. Do the different kinds of reflexes of different muscle systems tend to fall into certain patterns or combinations?

Discussion:
1. Do you suppose S's whole reaction to odors included other deeper reflexes unobservable by you? Name any which you think may have occurred. (Consider heart, stomach, "dizziness," etc.)
2. Do you find it easy or difficult to distinguish S's reactions into the two classes of "overt" and "implicit," or into "manual" and "visceral or emotional"?
3. To what extent do you think such patterns innate rather than acquired?

References: Dashiell, 193–98; Watson, 257–70; Hunter, 189–90.

XX. THE PSYCHOGALVANIC RESPONSE (Group)

Problem: To observe and measure the psychogalvanic response as a part of total emotional responses.

Materials: D'Arsonval galvanometer. Wheatstone bridge. 2 electrodes (nickel). A 6-volt battery. Switch. Wires for connection. A large graduated scale. Timer. Lamp. (Student to diagram arrangement of apparatus as actually used.)

Procedure: The room is darkened, and a narrow beam of very bright light from the lamp is adjusted to fall on the mirror of the galvanometer, from which it is reflected to the reading scale. S is blindfolded, and is seated by the electrodes. The two electrodes are placed on the palms or the backs of the two hands, or sometimes on the palm and back of one hand. They are bound on by means of bandaging tape, with a rubber band to give additional support. S's arm must be comfortably supported, and S should remain as quiet as possible. He should avoid all movements of the hands, as these may cause accidental changes in contact between the skin and the electrodes.

Close the circuits, and adjust the apparatus so that the beam of light falls on the zero point of the scale. It may be necessary to adjust the Wheatstone bridge, and also to change the poles of the batteries. *A trial may be made as follows:* When the initial galvanometric deflection has reached a reasonable stability, the E's note the reading on the scale. S is given the desired stimulus, and after a small latent time any new deflection which occurs is considered as the galvanic response, and is measured in terms of the number of degrees which the "spot" has moved on the scale. (After a few stimuli have been given, it may be desirable to bring the "spot" back to a convenient part of the scale. The body resistance of S is likely to vary in an unpredictable manner. This variance is a disturbing factor which can be partly controlled by changing the resistances in the Wheatstone bridge.)

A. Subject at Rest

The readings should be taken every 10 seconds for 2 or more minutes of quiescence. An assistant should signal these intervals with a small flash light or other signal not to be seen or heard by S.

B. Variety of Stimuli

The stimuli will be determined by the instructor, and will be displayed to the students at the time they are to be applied to S. In each trial, record the initial reading and also record readings every 10 seconds. By this means a fairly consistent graph may be secured which will portray what happened during every given stimulation.

Incidental (*a*). Note the general behavior of the "spot." Can you observe a slight negative deflection of the galvanometer when the stimulus is given? Try to estimate the latent period, or the time which elapses between the stimulus and the galvanic response. Is the progressive galvanometric excursion slow in returning to its original position?

Incidental (*b*). Repeat several times the stimuli which called out a marked galvanic response, and study the adaptation effect.

C. Word Association

The class records the stimulus words spoken by I, the responses evoked by S, and the time in fifths of seconds taken by the assistant with a stop watch, and especially the magnitude of the deflections when a galvanometric response occurs.

Results: E is to note down readings as they occur in a tabular form. E.g.:

For parts *A* and *B*:

NATURE OF STIMULUS	READING JUST BEFORE STIMULUS	SUCCESSIVE 10-SEC. READINGS AFTER STIMULUS	GREATEST READING	DEFLECTION
(none)	0	1, 0, 1.5, .5, 2, 1, ..	2	2
Creosote	1	9, 15, 13, 8, 4	15	14
Perfume	0	2, 2, 1.5, 1	2	2
Threat of pin	1.5	10, 8, 3.5	10	8.5
"Multiply 23 × 84"	0.5	6, 4, 11.5, 12, 8, 10	12	11.5
Loud noise	2	14, 20, 18.5, 11, 6.5	20	18
		(etc.)		

For part *C*:

STIMULUS WORD	RESPONSE WORD	READING BEFORE	GREATEST READING	DEFLECTION

47

Discussion:

1. This phenomenon is thought by some to be muscular in character; by others, to be circulatory; and by still others, to be perspiratory. For each explanation describe as definitely as you can the working of the effector mechanisms involved.
2. This phenomenon is sometimes called the "galvanic reflex." What other reflexes (of striped muscles, smooth muscles, duct glands, and ductless glands) can you name which probably occur as parts of the emotional responses to such stimuli as those used?
3. Rank the various stimuli applied under procedure B with reference to the intensity of the responses, and attempt some explanation of the ranking in terms of different degrees of importance of the stimuli to the organism.
4. Carefully inspect your records for part B, to seek any evidence *pro* or *con* on the question: Can the psychogalvanic response be used to reveal the kind of emotion aroused; e.g., anger, embarrassment, fear, etc. Present your evidence.

References: Dashiell, 214–15, 219–21, 221–22; Woodworth, 292–95; Perrin and Klein, 178–79; Hunter, 203–06; Pillsbury, 487–94.

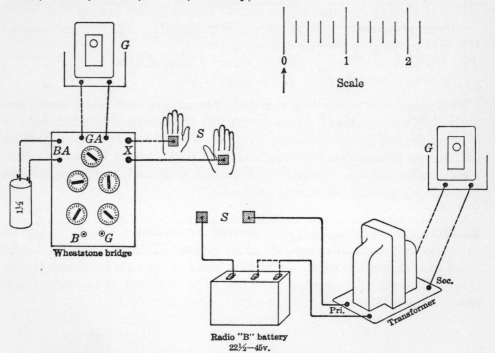

Two arrangements for the psychogalvanic experiment: (*A*) with Wheatstone bridge enclosed, (*B*) tachogram arrangement

XXI. CHANGES IN RESPIRATION AND PULSE IN DIFFERENT ACTIVITIES (Individual or Group)

Problem: (Student is to state this.)

Materials: Pneumograph. Sphygmograph. Recording tambour and tubing. Kymograph. Time marker. (Cf. Dashiell's text, Fig. 58, p. 216.)

Procedure: Let S be seated comfortably and breathing naturally. After I has carefully adjusted the pneumograph and sphygmograph and his assistant the recording pointers to the drum, the following situations are to be provided. They should continue for a uniform length of time (say, 20 sec.); and each should be preceded by an equal-length period of quiet, recorded as a "normal." The precise moments of the beginning of the stimulus (or special activity) and its cessation are to be indicated with vertical strokes on the drum, and the character of S's activity with "N," "I," "II," etc.

   I. S is to squeeze the hand dynamometer with rapidly repeated pulls.

  II. S is to keep his eyes closed and to attend to the ticking of a watch held so far away that he can scarcely hear it.

 III. S is to rehearse silently a familiar tune.

 IV. S is to read silently a page of material handed him.

  V. S is to submit to dermal pain stimulation.

  Pneumographic and sphygmographic records are best taken simultaneously, but may be taken separately, or the pneumographic taken only — it being the one more obviously affected. S must concentrate on his task (or, during Normal, on anything else) and forget about the instruments. I will readily think of alternative situations if desired, as having S listen to a stirring martial phonograph record.

Results: The pneumograph records after shellacking are to be analyzed: (*a*) as to frequency of cycles, (*b*) as to volume (distance from the lowest point of each inspiration to the highest point of the next following expiration). The sphygmograph records are to be analyzed as to frequency of beats. Cast results into tabular form. (See page 50.)

| ACTIVITY | TIME | RESPIRATION | | | | PULSE RATE | |
| | | RATE | | VOLUME | | | |
		Total cycles	Per min.	Total I–E's	Av. I–E	Total beats	Per. min.
Normal	20″	4.8	14.4	29.8 mm.	6.2 mm.	24.3	72.9
Dynamom.	20″	9.	27.	104.5	11.6	34.	102.
Listening	20″	5.3	15.9	21.2	4.	28.	84.

(etc.)

If a large group demonstration is used, the kymograph tracings can be posted under glass for the individual students to analyze later, or the raw data can later be furnished in tabulated form after an assistant has analyzed the tracings.

Discussion:

1. Compare the degree of sensitivity of these two visceral functions to variations in stimuli or situations.
2. Are changes in respiration always coincident with changes of heart beat? (Make definite references!) Are changes in rate of breathing always coincident with changes in depth of breathing, and with the same direction of such changes? Then, would you say that these visceral R's are linked together in an unvarying pattern?
3. What significance may your answers in 2 have for the question of emotional pattern-R's?

References: Dashiell, 215, 217, Fig. 58, 221; Titchener, 243–50; Woodworth, 292–94; Breese, 364–66; Perrin and Klein, 179.

XXII. ORGANIC DRIVE (Group)

Problem: To measure the degree to which a given physiological condition (hunger) determines overt behavior.

Materials: 10 white rats, 5 recently fed, 5 under at least 24 hours' hunger. Modified maze with criss-crossing pathways and without exit. Paper diagrams showing the maze, for tracing records, 10 to each student.

Procedure and Results: Take animals in alternating order: 1 fed, 1 hungry, 1 fed, 1 hungry, etc. Use the modified maze, introducing the animal at the door. For 90 seconds each individual is to keep accurate record of its movements by tracing its path with pencil on his diagram. Later, count the total number of "squares" each animal entered (at least with one forefoot); then make a table showing the results with all ten, and averages for "hungry" and for "fed." This method is a crude measure of general activity and of persistence; and can be used for studying activity under different degrees of hunger, of fatigue, of age, etc.

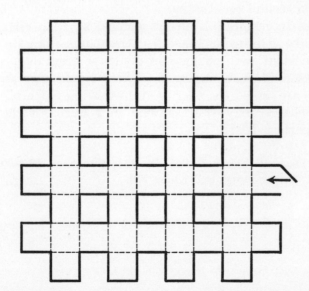

Discussion: State carefully how the experiment brings out:
1. The importance of the formula "$S \times O \longrightarrow R$." (Cf. Dashiell, p. 41.)
2. The importance of intero- and proprio-ceptors as compared with extero-ceptors.

51

3. The relations of inner "drive," "preparatory" R's, and "consummatory" R's.
4. Discuss the concept that one's "interests" have their foundations in, and are elaborations of, his "appetites."
5. Does your experiment show clearly whether the highly motivated activity involved has more the character of greater vigor or that of greater variation?   (Cf. Dashiell text, p. 242.)   Can you suggest some way of improving the experiment to differentiate these more clearly?
6. Consider the Dashiell text, Figures 62 and 63.   Which gives more evidence of the character of greater vigor, and which that of greater variation, in the highly motivated individual?

References: Dashiell, 232–42; Perrin and Klein, 140–47; Watson, note p. 292; Gates, 220–26; Woodworth, 228–29, 247 ff.

XXIII. ESTHETIC PREFERENCES (Individual or Group)

Problem: To measure some interests or motives by the method of Paired Comparisons. Incidentally, to determine some simple psychological principles of beauty.

Materials: A series of cards bearing colors or geometrical designs and lettered on the back. Harmonium, organ, or piano.

Procedure:

A. *Designs or Colors*

E or I is to present to S or S's the series of cards, exposing two at a time, side by side. If this is an individual experiment, S is to indicate which he prefers by pointing and E is to record. If it is a group experiment, I will announce at each presentation the letters by which the two cards are known, and each S will keep his individual record by entering in the appropriate square the letter of the preferred card.

For recording, use a record sheet of the following type:

	A	B	C	D	E	F	G	H	..	..	..	..	TOTAL PREFERENCES	FINAL RANKING
A	╳													
B		╳												
C			╳											
D				╳										
E					╳									
..						╳								
..							╳							

Each card is to be paired once with every other card in the series; the order being A with B, B with C, C with D, etc., then A with C, B with D, etc. (i.e., diagonally across and down the upper part of the diagram.) When a card is presented twice in succession shift its spatial position, as A (left) — B (right), B (left) — C (right).

53

The whole series should be gone through again and the results entered in the lower half of the record diagram.

B. Musical Intervals

E or I is to present a series of musical chords on an organ (or similar instrument) by sounding them in pairs. Each chord should be sustained a full two seconds and the silent interval between chords should not vary. E's pairing of the chords and S's recording of preferences is to be done in the same general manner as in A. Instead of announcing aloud the letters designating the chords about to be paired, E should have an assistant hold a pointer, before and during the presentation of the pair, on the appropriate square of a blank record diagram drawn on the blackboard.

This whole series should be gone through again at least once.

Results: For each experiment, S should total up the number of times each letter appears in the record diagram of preferences, and should rearrange in order of preference for the whole set (showing in parentheses the actual number of times each is preferred).

Class results are then totaled by I, first as a total of preferences for each card, then as rearranged to show class order of preference.

(For colors and chords.) I may also furnish to the class some results previously obtained with young school children.

Discussion:

A. (If designs are used.)

1. On the basis of your results with S (or the class results), what rules could you formulate for the psychology of beauty of closed geometrical designs especially with regard to these points:
   (a) best proportions of a rectangle (measure designs accurately),
   (b) balance,
   (c) angles or corners of different degrees,
   (d) rectilinear vs. rounded corners,
   (e) rectilinear vs. curved lines,
   (f) complex vs. simple figures.
   In the case of each rule name by letters the designs that are the basis of your conclusions.

2. Did your S's (or class average) choices among the rectangles approximate the "golden section" ($\frac{21}{34}$, or approximately $\frac{5}{8}$)? Measure the dimensions of many objects outside the laboratory — window pane, blotter, book, magazine page, envelope, desk top, etc. How many of them agree fairly well with the laboratory results?

(If colors are used.)

1. Does a careful scrutiny of your results tend to confirm or deny the assertion that the most preferred color combinations are based on complementaries and the least preferred involve hues lying somewhat but not very close together in the spectrum?
2. Study practical uses of color — in advertisements, in dress, etc. — to compare with your findings and also with the assertion in 1.
3. Compare the amount of agreement within your college-age group with the amount of agreement within the group of young children. If there are any differences, think out an explanation in genetic terms (to be found in chapter IX of Dashiell text).

B.

1. To what extent do your results agree with the relative frequency with which different tonal intervals are employed in musical composition? Are the least preferred ever used? Explain. (Consider classical Ger-

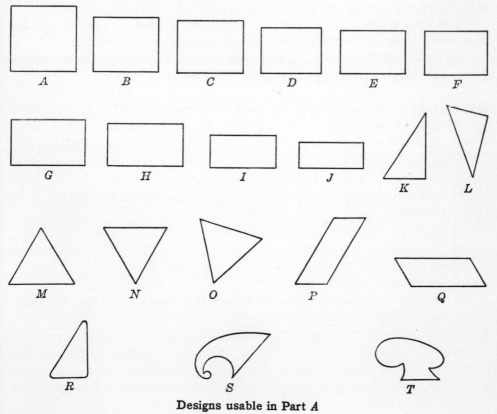

Designs usable in Part A

55

man music as compared with modernistic Russian or with American jazz.)

2. Centuries ago the octave was regarded most highly; but not today. Explain.
3. Apply question *A*, 3 to part *B* of the experiment.

General.
1. Which of the two methods of measuring strength of motivation in animals resembles more closely your present experiment? In the world of art appreciation is there anything resembling the other method?
2. May evidences of artistic motives or interests be obtained by wholly non-verbal methods?
3. In this experiment you have studied the measuring of esthetic interests or values. Are similar methods used (technically or non-technically) to measure ethical values? Economic? Intellectual?

References: Dashiell, 104–05, 109–11, 256–57, 417–20; Titchener, 241–43; Robinson and Robinson, 546–47, 558–59; Woodworth, 406–07; Gates, 171–80.

XXIV. MOTIVATION: VOCATIONAL INTERESTS (Group)

Problem: To measure the directions and strengths of interests of manifold types, and to analyze their bearing upon occupational choice, by the method of the "interest blank."

Materials: Individual copies of Strong's "vocational interest blank." Scoring scales for several vocations.

Procedure: I distributes the blanks and gives general instructions. Students proceed to answer the questionnaire, working rapidly and marking down their first impressions.

When a student's blank is finished, he is given the scales for scoring it for one profession, and for finally rating it. If time permits, the scales for a second or a third vocation are similarly used. At the end of the scoring all scales are to be carefully returned to I.

Results and Discussion:
1. To what extent do you suppose a person's original physiological equipment of capacities is responsible for his occupational choice, and to what extent are his socially acquired sentiments responsible?
2. Enumerate several kinds of social influences that affect vocational choice.
3. Do occupational interests tend to be permanent through the early 'teens? The latter 'teens? Outline a method for determining this scientifically.
4. Why do you suppose such a long and detailed questionnaire is used?
5. "The ratings assigned one in different vocations on results of this test are based on empirical data." What is meant by this?

References: Dashiell, 256; Watson, 419–24.

(*Note.* An excellent alternative exercise (for group or home work) is easily arranged for the measurement of personal attitudes on certain social problems (the church, war, the Negro, etc.) by the use of scales developed by Thurstone and others. The above questions are readily adapted to this test. The test would serve appropriately also in connection with discussions of social behavior.)

XXV. MOTIVATION: DETECTION OF HIDDEN CONFLICT
(GROUP)

Problem: To obtain objective evidence of a conflict between incompatible motivated behavior-tendencies, as provided in a case of guilty knowledge.

Materials: List of stimulus words, crucial and non-crucial. Stop watch. Sphygmomanometer and stethoscope. (Cf. Dashiell, Fig. 58, p. 216.)

Procedure: I has provided an envelope containing instructions to perpetrate certain acts or perform certain stunts in or about the building in which the class is meeting. Two class members are chosen to leave the room and to decide between themselves which one is to serve as the "innocent" and which the "guilty" S. The former waits in a near-by room while the latter opens his envelope and goes through with the performances demanded therein. When finished, he rejoins the "innocent" S; and they await summonses from the "court." (The "innocent" S is, of course, to remain in ignorance of anything the "guilty" one has done.) The acts demanded of the "guilty" man should be of critical and emotion-arousing character involving mislaying, "stealing," or "defacing" of property, addressing people or performing foolishly before them, etc. — acts he might ordinarily hesitate to perform and would be loath to confess, yet will remember.

Meanwhile, I reads to the group a copy of the instructions given the "guilty" S, and then exhibits a (previously covered) list of 50 or 75 common words on the blackboard. Of these, 25 are closely related to the details of the "crime" (crucial words), and are distributed singly and in groups of 2 to 4 among the 25 or 50 others (non-crucial). The crucial words are underscored.

A summons to the waiting S's brings one into the room. He is seated facing the class. I speaks the first word of the list and starts his stop watch, S responds as quickly as he can with the very first word which occurs to him, or with a substitute if he prefers, and I stops the watch. So on through the list. Members of the class copy each stimulus word, response word, and reaction time, as it is posted on the blackboard by an assistant to I. The class must not disturb S in any way!

The other S is now brought in for similar examination.

Blood pressure readings should be taken with a sphygmomanometer by I or assistant, on each S (a) *before* he leaves the room in the beginning, (b) when first brought back for examination before class, (c) half-way through the word-association series, or oftener, (d) at the end of the series.

Results: Tabulate your results in the following form, taking them from the blackboard where I or his assistant will post them during the experiment:

	1st subject				2d subject			
stim. word	resp. word	time	dev. from avg.	B P	resp. word	time	dev. from avg.	B P
(before leaving room)				127				130
(before examination)				133				131
"door"	"slam"	2.4	.6		"knob"	1.8	.2	
"chalk"	"write"	1.6	.2					
(half through exam.)				135				128

(etc.)

Find the average and the average deviation of the reaction times to the crucial words; to the non-crucial. Using these as well as other diagnostic signs (cf. Dashiell text, p. 222), determine whether you have evidence that either S was showing conflict and inhibition of responses.

Compare the successive blood pressure readings, as to their regularity, especially as compared with the first one taken before the S's left the room. The critical indication is not the absolute height of the readings but their regularity.

When all results have been scrutinized by the group, ask the members to vote as to the "guilty" S. Check by confessions of the S's.

Discussion:
1. Explain, so far as possible on a psychological basis, all the evidences of deception (or repression) used. What does each tend to show?
2. Explain the advantage of presenting some crucial words in immediate succession instead of singly.
3. Criticize this as a method of proving guilt or innocence.
4. How might it be adapted to the examination of abnormal (neurotic and psychotic or "insane") people?
5. Enumerate other methods that are probably of use in detecting conflict.

References: Dashiell, 216–17, 221–23, 260–63, 561; Perrin and Klein, 175–78; Woodworth, 429–31; Gates, 534–36; Watson, 227–31.

59

XXVI. INFLUENCE OF EMOTIONAL DISTRACTION ON OVERT ACTIVITIES (INDIVIDUAL OR GROUP)

Problem: (Student is to state the problem.)

Materials: The same materials as in the experiments TESTS OF MANUAL DEXTERITY and WORK AND FATIGUE IN SEMI-IMPLICIT ACTIVITY. Cancellation test blanks.

Procedure:

The General Method

E is to compare S's efficiency on each of several tests, (*a*) under *normal* conditions, and (*b*) under conditions of *emotional distraction*.

The tests: — For *simple overt* activities use

                (*A*) the hand dynamometer,
                (*B*) the tapping board,
                (*C*) the coördination plate,
                (*D*) the tracing test.

These have all been described and the procedures to be followed have been given in detail in TESTS OF MANUAL DEXTERITY, pp. 13–15, to which the student should again refer.

For *more complex semi-implicit* activities use

(*E*) a cancellation test. S is to be furnished with a printed page (face down), and at a signal from E or I is to turn it over and as he reads it left to right and line by line he is to cancel out with a pencil a certain letter previously named by E every time it occurs on the page. The cancelling is done by striking a short oblique line through the letter. The total time required for cancelling the given letter every time it occurs on the page is to be noted by E.

(*F*) a computation test. Use here the cumulative adding material and method described in the experiment, WORK AND FATIGUE IN SEMI-IMPLICIT ACTIVITY; but use only 2 or 3 of the columns.

A little preliminary practice to acquaint S with his tasks may be advisable, especially for (*E*) and (*F*). In these two cases use for practice letters and numbers other than those to be used in the formal tests.

Under Normal Conditions

The tests described above are to be administered to S, one after the other, under normal or usual laboratory conditions without any disturbing emotional or attention-distracting stimuli. In both this and the following set of tests it will be essential that E or I administer them and make his recordings as accurately as he can, otherwise no profitable comparison of the two series will be possible.

Under Special Conditions

The same tests are now to be administered to S under unusual conditions, conditions likely to have emotion-arousing or attention-distracting value. Consider those used in THE PSYCHOGALVANIC RESPONSE.

Results: Tabulate your data to show in parallel columns the results obtained for each test in the two different kinds of situations. If a variety of stimuli are used for the emotional distractions, indicate which is used in each case. More definite differences may appear when S has been tested more than once under each of the two kinds of conditions; or when his results are grouped with those of other S's.

Discussion:
1. Why are not your special conditions called simply "emotional" or simply "distracting"? Are these two qualities involved in equal degrees in your different special conditions?
2. Do your findings tend to confirm the view of the relations of emotions to activity as suggested in Figure 64 of the Dashiell text?
3. Were the effects of emotional distractions more evident in the vigor or in the accuracy of the functions tested? More evident on tho grosser or on the subtler functions?
4. If several special stimuli were used, did they all affect S's activities in the same direction?
5. Some of your tests were conducted by the time-limit method, some by the work-limit. What advantage is there to each method?

References: Dashiell, 211–13, 246–48, 270–72, 299; Watson, 215–18, 244–49; Pillsbury, 276–77, 500–01; Gates, 205–10.

XXVII. MOTOR ATTITUDE IN ATTENDING
(Individual or Group)

Problem: To determine some of the motor activities involved in an attentive posture.

Materials: Automatograph.

A. Non-Instrumental Observation

Procedure: S is to attend closely and in concentrated manner to some source of stimulation, and E is to note whatever motor activities (both phasic and postural) S is making while so attending. Afterward, S is to add his own observations of his motor activities during the attending.

As tasks for S, use:

A. Listening for a very faint sound, as of a watch held at a distance.

B. Trying to see clearly the irregularities in the shape of the period at the end of this sentence.

C. Thinking of the names of the eight most important events in American history in the order of their importance.

On each task make repeated trials to get as accurate and detailed an analysis as possible.

Important: S should be as natural and naïve as possible in these tasks: he must not seek to hide movements from E.

For group work, the class may be divided into pairs as they are seated; or naïve S's, preferably children, may be examined before the class without knowing the object of the experiment.

Results: In each trial, record in as great detail as you can both what E and what S could observe in the way of motor adjustments. Consider such different kinds as:

1. Muscles associated with the receptors involved.
2. Diffuse muscular tensions.
3. Changes in respiration, circulation, etc.

B. Instrumental Observation

Procedure: S stands blindfolded with one side to a table, his arm free from his body, and his hand resting lightly and easily upon an automatograph placed upon the table. I's (or E's) assistant takes up positions in various parts of the room for a few moments each, addressing simple questions to S. I (E) carefully marks a tiny cross, to show the position of the pointer each time the assistant changes his place. If the complete record is a good one I should be able to show what parts of it were made when the assistant stood at S's left, etc.

Results: An accurate quantitative analysis of the graphic record will usually not be possible. Make a preliminary analysis of your paper copy of the record by marking off with dotted lines of different colors the areas in which tracings were made during the different respective directions of stimulation of S by the assistant.

1. Is there any spatial or directional correspondence between the type of stimulation and the character of S's arm movements?
2. Which of the three kinds of motor adjustments, mentioned in *A. Results*, is responsible for your results here?

Discussion:
1. What do you suggest as the basis for the "effort" in attention?
2. Why and how do you suppose close attending produces "fatigue" or tiredness?
3. Is it easy or difficult to determine what a young child is attending to? An adult? In the latter case, must we ever assume that no motor adjustments are being made at all?
4. Delicate instrumentation will bring to light each class of muscular change listed under *A. Results*. Name at least one kind of apparatus that might be employed for each of the three classes, besides the automatograph.

References: Dashiell, 285–89, 398, 451–53; Pillsbury, 268–72; Breese, 81–84; Woodworth, 300–07.

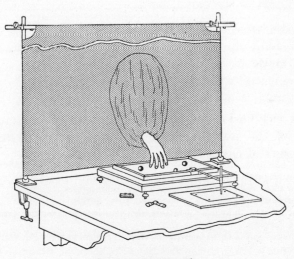

An automatograph

63

XXVIII. FACTORS IN ATTRACTING ATTENTION
(INDIVIDUAL OR GROUP)

Problem: To identify some of the conditions that determine what stimuli will be attended to.

Materials: Tachistoscope. Different series of exposure cards bearing letters in different arrangements. (Cf. Dashiell, Fig. 67, p. 294.)

Procedure: Using the tachistoscope E (I) presents to the S's the cards of set I, one at a time. Each exposure is preceded by a "ready" signal and the announcement of the index number of the card. Immediately after the exposure the characters on the card are to be reproduced as completely as possible by the S's on record paper, opposite the index number announced by E.

The experiment is continued with cards of sets II, III, IV, V.[1]

Results: S is to compare his reproductions with the original cards later exhibited by E; and is to construct a table:

Set	Kind of letters or words	Total on all cards	No. correctly noticed on all cards	Per cent noticed
I	large	. . . .	. . . .	. . . .
	small	. . . .	. . . .	. . . .
II	. . . .	. . . .	. . . .	. . . .
	. . . .	. . . .	. . . .	. . . .

(etc.)

Discussion:

1. Considering the various objective and subjective factors mentioned in any one of the texts listed below, state which is brought out in each of the sets of cards used.

[1] E's (I's) cards to be prepared in advance by I as follows:
(I) 1 set of four or more each bearing 4 large and 4 small letters (black).
(II) 1 set of four or more each bearing 6 black and 2 red letters.
(III) 1 set of four or more each bearing 4 letters identical in character and position on successive cards with 4 varying.
(IV) 1 set of six or more, half of them bearing 8 letters in nonsense arrangement, the others bearing 8-letter words.
(V) 1 set of four or more, bearing words closely resembling other words, and to be introduced with a spoken series.
(N.B.: S should not know in advance in what order these sets will be used.)

2. Describe how experiments might be arranged to exhibit those factors not brought out here.
3. Do any of the sets bring out any of the three rôles of postures in behavior? Show how.
4. What two principles brought out in this experiment throw light on the function of the chorus to a song, and to a Greek play?
5. Which principles are used by the magician?

References: Dashiell, 279–84, 289–93; Pillsbury, 277–84; Hunter, 303–08; Woodworth, 368–72; Perrin and Klein, 79–80; Warren and Carmichael, 69–70.

XXIX. ATTENDING: SIMULTANEOUS ACTIVITIES
(Individual or Group)

Problem: To investigate methods by which one carries on two disparate activities simultaneously.

Materials: Blank writing paper.

Procedure: (For a group experiment: have individuals paired as they are seated, so that one, acting as S, can be observed by the other sitting to his right or left as E.)

A

(a) S is to speak in undertones as fast as possible, the *alternate letters* of the alphabet, A, C, E, G, etc. When he reaches Z, he is to begin at A again, and so continue calling the alternate letters until stopped by E at the end of 1 min. E is to keep count of the number of letters called. (He can do this by making pencil strokes as E calls.)

(b) S is to write down, as fast as possible, every *third number* beginning with 1, 4, 7, 10, etc. When he reaches 100 he is to begin at 1 again, and so continue until stopped at the end of 1 min. E can obtain the total from the written page.

(c) S is now to try to perform *both* operations at once, speaking the alternate letters and writing the third numbers simultaneously, and continuing until stopped at the end of 1 min.

B

(a), (b), (c) With the same S repeat the three procedures described above except that for (a) S should speak the *successive letters*, A, B, C, D, etc., and for (b) he should write the *successive numbers*, 1, 2, 3, etc.

Results and Discussion:
1. Compare the amount of work done in A (c) with that done in A (a) and in A (b).

If S were able to perform the two operations (speaking alternate letters and writing third numbers) at once, without one's interfering with the other in any way, how should the results of (c) compare with those of (a) and of (b)? On the other hand, if S were able to oscillate perfectly between the two operations, how would (c) compare with (a) and (b)? What do your findings indicate?

2. Similarly compare the amount of work done in B (c) with that done in B (a) and B (b).

3. How do you explain any significant difference between answers to 1 and to 2?

References: Dashiell, 295–97; Woodworth, 375–78; Gates, 376–77; Watson, 312–14.

XXX. FLUCTUATIONS IN ATTENDING (Individual or Group)

Problem: To measure fluctuations of attention; and to observe some causes of them.

Materials: A figure in reversible perspective.

Procedure: The figure is placed in an upright position before S or S's. S fixates the line *ab* and tries to see the cube with side *abcd* nearer than the side *efgh*. He then fixates *gh* and tries to reverse the figure bringing *efgh* nearer. When he can reverse the figure at will, he is ready to proceed with the experiment.

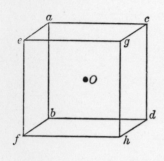

A. S looks at the figure for 1 min. (time kept by E) passively, allowing his eyes to roam at will over the figure. He tries neither to make nor to inhibit reversals. In the individual form of the experiment S calls out each reversal that does occur, and E records by making a short pencil stroke for each, then totaling them for the minute; in the group form, S will have to keep pencil to paper and make his own recording strokes without looking at them. Three trials are made.

B. Proceed as in method *A* except that S tries to make as *many* reversals as possible by looking at *ab* and *gh* alternately. Three 1 min. trials are made.

C. Proceed as before except that S fixates the dot *O* and tries to *hold* the figure in one position, recording the number of reversals which occur in spite of his effort. Three 1 min. trials are made. S notices any eye-movements which may occur, and their relation to the reversals of the figure.

A rest of one half minute should be given between the successive trials, and five minute rests between the three parts, *A*, *B*, and *C*. In the individual experiment repeat with S and E interchanged.

Results:
1. Present a table showing the number of reversals for the three different methods, *A*, *B*, and *C*, with the average for each method.
2. Can S report any eye-movements or any unusual variations in the appearance of the figure which he observed in method *C*?

Discussion:
1. Explain the phenomenon of reversal as observed in method A.
2. How would you say the rapid reversals of method B were obtained?
3. What do you consider the cause or causes of the reversals in method C?
4. What general principle is brought out by comparing results of A and C; and what practical application can be made of it?

References: Dashiell, 297–99; Breese, 70–76; Titchener, 291–93; Pillsbury, 274–76; Woodworth, 385–88; Warren and Carmichael, 74–75; Hunter, 312–15.

XXXI. INTELLIGENCE TESTS; INDIVIDUAL DIFFERENCES
(GROUP)

Problem: Two of the most important contributions of modern psychology are the development of reliable methods of measuring intelligent behavior, and the scientifically exact study of individual differences in capacities. Our problem: To take some examples (incomplete) of the former, and to treat them in terms of the latter.

Materials: Test blanks (provided by I).   (Name the tests.)

Procedure and Results: The tests are to be given by I to the whole class.   Each individual is to score his own results.   These scores for the whole class are to be reported on the blackboard, and the individual is to copy them.

These group results are to be treated statistically.   On each test, first tabulate the class scores in two columns, to show the order of scores made from lowest to highest, and the number of individuals making each score. Then draw graphs, using distances on the base line to show the scores and vertical distances to show the numbers of individuals.   Make a separate curve for each test.

Find the coefficient of correlation between 1st and 2d tests; between 2d and 3d tests; between 3d and 4th tests.

Discussion:
1. Do the group curves found show any resemblance at all to the shape of the normal distribution curve?   What if the class had been larger?
2. On a distribution curve for general intelligence, where would you expect to find the geniuses; the idiots?   How would you compare them in number of individuals with the population average?
3. Does high capacity in one trait tend to go with high capacity in others? What evidence on this do you find from your coefficients of correlation?
4. "Even if our selections of tests were complete for measuring intelligence they would not give us all we want to know about human nature." Expand this.

References: Dashiell, 313–15, 562–67; Woodworth, 34–37, 63–69; Hunter, 80, 88–91; Perrin and Klein, 324–31, 340–45; Warren and Carmichael, 342–50; Gates, 456–57, 464, 504–05; Robinson and Robinson, 722–31, 737–50, 762–67.

XXXII. JUDGING INTELLIGENCE BY APPEARANCE
(INDIVIDUAL OR GROUP)

Problem: Is a person's degree of intelligence easily determined by observing his appearance?

A

Materials: 12 photographs of children. Table of I.Q. measurements (not to be seen until experimental work is completed).

Procedure: After studying the photographs one by one S is to select the child which to him appears to be the *brightest*, i.e., the most intelligent for his age. This photograph is to be placed at the extreme left. If at first several appear about equally bright, he should set them aside and use a brief method of paired comparisons (Dashiell text, pp. 256–57) to determine their final ranking. S is then to pick the second brightest; and place it on the right and next to the first; the third brightest; and so on. When all have been arranged in a final order-of-merit array, S should again go through the series to see if each child looks brighter than the one on the right, duller than the one on the left. If not the list is to be revised accordingly.

Results: The table of I.Q.'s is now to be consulted. These were obtained by careful individual examinations of the twelve children photographed. A record table should be made as follows:

Pictures, by letter	Ranks assigned	I.Q.'s	True ranking

1. In general, are S's judgments in fairly close agreement with the known I.Q.'s? What is the coefficient of correlation?
2. The rankings made by the other members of the group are to be posted side by side, and the average rank for each picture determined. Each S is to determine the correlation between his own ranking and that of the group average. Compare with the answer to 1.
3. The correlation coefficients for other members of the group are to be posted and copied; and S is to find the median and the average of these.

Discussion:

1. State carefully any conclusion suggested by the comparison of results on questions 1 and 2.
2. Do you think judgments based upon sight of the actual children would be more accurate? Why?
3. Discuss critically the value of the photograph which is often demanded with applications for positions.

B

Materials (subjects): Several children whose I.Q.'s are known to the instructor.

Procedure: The children are to be viewed by the class under different conditions such as the following:

(*a*) *Passive posture.* They are to sit in a row facing the class while I takes occasion to address them or the class on some casual topics.

(*b*) *Active posture.* I engages their attention with a dramatic story, sleight-of-hand trick, a new mechanical toy, etc.

(*c*) *Reading aloud.* They are to read selected passages.

(*d*) *Interview.* Questions of uniform routine types are asked each child.

Under *each* of the conditions for observing the children, the class members are to make out a ranking for their relative brightness, trying to construct each ranking on the basis of *that* observation only.

Results:

1. (For each S.) Which method of observing yielded judgments most nearly approaching the order of I.Q.'s obtained by testing?
2. For each of the observation methods the ranking by the members of the class are to be averaged and compared with the test results.
3. The A.D.'s of the class ranking by each method may be computed. What additional light is thus furnished?

Discussion:

1. Referring to each observation-condition separately, describe as many as possible of the cues that operated to influence your judgment of brightness: neatness of dress, smiling, attentive notice of students, smooth voice, inflections, bright eye, quickness in speaking, etc., etc.
2. Discuss critically the value of the photograph of an applicant for a job. Of an interview with him.

References: Dashiell, Fig. 69 and note, p. 307; Gates, 405–08; Watson, 426–27.

XXXIII. TESTS OF MUSICAL APTITUDES (Group)

Problem: To measure certain auditory capacities, or musical traits.

Materials: Set of phonograph disks devised by Seashore. Distribution curves on wall charts. Record blanks.

Procedure: Class demonstration. I will play the disks, preceding each by oral instructions. Students are to attend and to mark their blanks as per instructions.

        1. Discrimination of pitch.
        2. Discrimination of intensity.
        3. Estimation of time.
        4. Tonal memory.
        5. Discrimination of rhythm.

Results:
1. Score each blank by means of the key read by the instructor. Get the total rights on each blank and find the percentage score $\left(\dfrac{R}{T}\right)$. Copy the distribution curves shown by I or posted in the laboratory. Locate the point for your percentage score on each by drawing a vertical line through the base line and through the curve.
2. If available, record and show on curves the average percentage scores of the class.

Discussion:
1. The five elements are held to be innate talents or capacities and as such not improvable. But older children make better scores than younger: to what psychological factors can the difference be due?
2. Name some other human capacities that you think should be added to these to make a complete series of tests for musical talent.
3. Which of the five elements in this demonstration are involved in understanding spoken language? Give one example in each case, e.g., how rise and fall in pitch conveys some of speaker's meaning.
4. The first three tests involve a "threshold" problem that is one of those attacked by the "psychophysical" methods. Which?
5. In threshold determination a common error is that of the "absolute impression": in the course of a series of judgments, S comes to judge no longer by comparing simply the two stimuli being presented at a

given time but by comparing one or the other with a lasting set which is becoming established in him. Could this error be detected in the responses to tests 1 or 2?

References: Dashiell, 113–17, 320; Gates, 484–87; Hunter, 87–88; Perrin and Klein, 334–35, 358; Robinson and Robinson, 738–42.

XXXIV. HABIT FORMATION: MIRROR DRAWING (INDIVIDUAL)

Problem: To study the rate and some of the factors of improvement in a manual activity by trial and error.

Materials: Mirror. Screen. Series of 22 printed stars. Watch with second hand.

Procedure: Set up the mirror in such a way that the reflection of the hand is visible when you are seated with the hand in a writing position on the table. Adjust the screen so as to cut off direct vision of the hand, but not its reflection in the mirror. Place the card containing the star with its edge square with edge of the table, and the cross-line that indicates the starting-point at the back. Place the tip of your pencil on the cross-line of the star. You are to trace the outline of the star, starting toward the right and continuing clockwise until the starting-point is reached. You must try to keep on the line, and must keep the pencil going continually in the same direction, returning to the line whenever it is left. Keep the pencil on the paper all the time. The time is to be taken with the watch and written below the star.

An error record is later to be made out as follows: Carefully examine each tracing, and count one error for each corrective movement, i.e., for each attempt, when the pencil was off the line, to return to it. If several turns were made before the line was successfully reached, count each such turn that was made toward the line as the evidence of an error.

Make the first trial in the mirror with the *left* hand. Mark this blank *L 1*. Follow this by twenty trials with the *right* hand, numbering cards *1* to *20*. Finally, make a drawing with the left hand in the mirror, and mark this *L 2*.

Results: Make a table showing time and errors for each trial. Draw learning curves of times and of errors for the 20 successive tracings made with the right hand and the mirror, using a black line for time and a red one for errors. Note the form of the curve.

Discussion:
1. Name some other acts that you can think of which are secured by the method of trial and error.
2. Is there any change in the method of afferent control (visual, kines-

75

thetic, etc.) of movements as the experiment continues? Is there the forming of a serial habit?

3. How far do rational processes aid in the formation of such habits?
4. What effect did practice with the right hand have on the left hand? Refer to your data.
5. Are any plateaus shown in either time or error curve?

References: Dashiell, 332, 339–48, 351–53; Woodworth, 141–42; Hunter, 286–87; Robinson and Robinson, 142–43, 152–57, 170–74; Perrin and Klein, 243–48, 257–67; Gates, 308–14, 320–27.

XXXV. HABIT FORMATION: MAZE RUNNING (INDIVIDUAL)

Problem: To measure the development of a hierarchy as a complex serial habit involving habit units of different levels of complexity.

Materials: Two stylus mazes. Stylus. Watch. Screen. Blank sheets of paper. Pencil.

Procedure: Maze A is to be used with one person acting as S, Maze B with the other. Do not look at the mazes until ready for the experiment, and each subject is not to see his own maze at all.

Learning a maze consists in learning to run through the true passageway without making false turns into blind alleys nor reversing direction on the true path. The rate of learning in successive trials is measured by the reduction in the number of errors made and by the reduction in the time required to run from entrance to exit. In the stylus maze small grooves are used for the passageways and S traverses them with a stylus or pointer, using no other aids but 'feeling' with the stylus.

E, sitting across the table, is to set S's maze before him (S not looking) so that the entrance (end of groove closed with a block) lies directly in front of the midline of his body. A screen is fixed above the maze to shut off S's vision of it, and another screen conceals E's record (or else, S is blindfolded). S is then to take the stylus in his fingers much as he would a pencil but holding it vertical, and not placing his fingers below the guard. As S holds the stylus E should insert its point at the beginning of the groove against the stop block. At a signal "go," E starts his watch, and S begins moving the stylus along the groove until it finally goes off the edge of the whole board. E immediately stops the watch. S must remember: Never lift the stylus from the floor of the groove; always keep the stylus in a strictly vertical position; never let the fingers or hand touch the maze at any point. S is not to see E's records.

Repeat for a total of 25 trials or until 2 errorless runs in succession are made. *After each 5 trials* S is to be given a pencil and a blank sheet of paper on which to reproduce by free-hand drawing the path of the maze as well as he can recall it. His eyes are to be closed and he is not to see his drawings until the whole experiment is finished. The drawing is to be full size.

Results: Records are to be taken by E on ruled paper during the trial, using one line for each trial.

Sample Records:

Trial	Errors	Time
1	A C F R B D G H R J	87″
2	B C F G R R H I J	43″

In recording errors use appropriate letters for the particular blind alleys entered as they appear printed on the maze, and "R" for each return or reversed direction on the true path. Record every error as soon as it is made.

Plot results of the total number of trials on one graph, using a black line for time, a red line for errors.

Discussion: Habit-forming involves the establishing not only of inclusive (higher order) habits, but also of particular (lower order) habits.

1. What is the highest unit habit here, the most inclusive?
2. Lower order habits here would be the particular turns and runs that go in to make up the whole. From a study of your records name certain errors that the subject easily avoided; name others that were hard to avoid.
3. The lower order habits referred to in 2 were serial or successive in nature. Name one or two that were involved in S's behavior at the *same time* (such as, correct holding of stylus). Did you happen to notice any improvement in these?
4. Some investigators have asserted that the lower order (integral) habits must first be well fixed before progress with the higher order (combinations) occurs; others say that both lower and higher units of response are developed at the same time. After comparing your record of errors with the subject's successive attempts to draw free-hand the whole maze course, express some opinion on this question.
5. Does the drop in your time curve indicate only the elimination of time-wastes in errors or does it indicate also a real increase in speed of moving? Is the latter to be expected usually with increased familiarity and accuracy of movement in learning an act? Give an example from everyday life.

References: Dashiell, 330–31, 347–51; Woodworth, 126–29, 131–37; Perrin and Klein, 205–15, 243–48; Gates, 308–14; Pillsbury, 510–12; Robinson and Robinson, 160–64.

XXXVI. HABIT FORMATION: SUBSTITUTION (GROUP)

Problem: To measure the rate of improvement in an activity and to measure certain interrelations between habits.

Materials: Substitution blanks, bearing at the top codes of digits paired with letters.

Procedure: 11 blanks are distributed face down to each student. At a signal from I each student is to turn over his top blank and immediately proceed to work at high speed on the task of writing under each digit the letter which appears under that same digit in the code at the top of the sheet. "Stop" will be called by I at the end of a definite period (3, 4, or 5 min.). The same general type of performance is to be repeated on each of the remaining blanks.

Students will score their papers for errors either in class time from I's reading or at other times by consulting correct blanks posted conveniently.

Results and Discussion:

A. Results for the Individual

Each student will tabulate his errors and his time for each successive trial; and will then draw on the same coördinates graphs to show his individual curves of acquiring, using black ink for times and red for errors.
1. Does the time curve show positive or negative acceleration?
2. Does it show short irregular fluctuations? If so, to what do you ascribe these? Answer carefully.
3. Does it show a plateau?
4. Do the number of errors and the total time seem to vary together, inversely, or independently? Explain the result carefully.
5. Is this learning by trial and error? Show explicitly.

B. Results for the Group

The student now is to reduce his error and time scores to one set of scores. One method of doing this is as follows: for every incorrect substitution add to the total time the average time taken for one substitution.

The individual weighted-time records are then totaled and averaged trial by trial in or out of class in 3 groups: S, those working on the same code throughout, except the last; C, those working on codes changing completely from trial to trial; I, those working on codes partly identical and partly changed from trial to trial, except the last. The tabulation

79

of these 3 series of group averages is to be copied from the blackboard by the student.

The student will draw curves for the S, C, I methods on one graph; and draw conclusions from them.

1. How would you compare the curves to show how the phenomenon of interference was involved in the task of one group? Formulate a statement, then, as to just what relationships between two habits make for interference.
2. Which is more rapidly learned, one identical performance or a series of similar ones? Which is the more effective training for meeting future demands for similar (not identical) performances?
3. Generalize this point as bearing on the question of transfer of training.
4. Analyze and state as precisely as you can *just what* are the likenesses and differences between tasks S and C. Consider: "higher and lower level habits," "hierarchy," "reaction patterns."

References: Dashiell, 348–55; Woodworth, 124–31; Hunter, 284–87, 296–98; Robinson and Robinson, 142–43, 152–70; Perrin and Klein, 248–67; Gates, 314–18, 320–27; Pillsbury, 510–20.

XXXVII. HABIT FORMATION: TRANSFERENCE AND INTERFERENCE (INDIVIDUAL OR GROUP)

Problem: To identify and measure the effects of one habit upon the learning of another, similar but not identical.

Materials: Two packs of "flinch" cards. Card sorting tray.

Procedure (for individual method): When E has the tray arranged and the pack ready, S is to take the pack in his hand face up and sort the cards as they come into their proper pigeon holes as marked on the tray. He should sort as fast as possible, and E should note and record the precise amount of time taken for the sorting of the complete pack (from the instant the first card is taken off the pack in the hand to the instant the last card is placed in its compartment). In case S places a card in the wrong compartment he is to correct the error before continuing. Use lay-out A for a total of 12 successive sortings, then lay-out B for 6, then A again for 6.

While S is dealing one pack E shuffles the other. E and S exchange rôles; and repeat the experiment.

(Variation for group or home-work method.) Take ten slips of paper and number them from "1" to "10." Place these on a desk before you about 4 to 6 in. apart, in two rows of five each, but with the numbers in a chance order (don't observe the order closely!). Hold in the hand face up a shuffled pack of cards ("flinch," "rook," or playing cards with J, Q, and K removed), and sort them as fast as possible to the various numbers. Take note of the precise time by a watch at the beginning and ending of the sorting.

Continue for 12 successive sortings, shuffling well between sortings. Then make a new chance lay-out for 6 sortings, and finally return to the original lay-out for 6.

Results: Record the times in tabular form as follows:

Trial	Time
1	310 sec.
2	221 "
3	207 "
4	(etc.)

Graph the time scores shown in your table in the form of a learning curve and indicate the points at which S shifted from one lay-out to another by leaving a break in your curve.

Discussion:

1. How do the three series compare, especially as to first, middle, and last trials?

2. Does habit *A* appear to assist or to interfere or both with the formation of habit *B*? What evidences of this do you find from your table and graph?

3. If practice on both habits were continued indefinitely would you expect to find any difference in the amount of assistance or interference?

4. Name two habits from your own experience one of which helped in the forming of the other (transference). Name two that interfered. Name two that had neither effect on each other.

References: Dashiell, 353–55; Hunter, 284–87; Perrin and Klein, 280–84; Robinson and Robinson, 168–70; Watson, 310–11, 361.

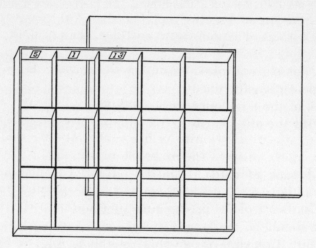

Card sorting tray with removable bottom

XXXVIII. MEMORIZING: ROTE *vs.* MEANINGFUL
(Individual or Group)

Problem: To study the effect of meaningfulness as a factor influencing both the rate of acquiring and retention.

Materials: Lists of words and syllables in envelopes. Watch. For the individual experiment, also an exposure device, and bell-metronome set to ring at 2-sec. intervals. (Cf. Dashiell, Fig. 101, p. 498.)

Procedure:

A. (As an Individual experiment)

Two complete sets of lists are provided, to be used by the two individuals of the working pair, respectively.[1]

E must first familiarize himself with the exposure device; and should practice (without S's looking) presenting the successive items of the list through the aperture. Practice making the shift from item to item smoothly, and with good exposures, at each bell sound from the metronome.

In the experiment itself, S is to attend closely and attempt at the end of a series to reproduce all the items in correct order. E is to repeat the whole list again and again, until a perfect reproduction is made by S, and is to keep note of the number of such repetitions made.

Continue with the other cards in like manner, after brief rests.

B. (As a Group or home experiment)

One set of lists is provided.[1] Do not open the envelope beforehand! The experiment is to be conducted by you as both E and S. For this work be sure to find a place free from distractions.

The student should be instructed to prepare a "shutter" by cutting a rectangular aperture from card or paper. This is to be used by the left hand, sliding it down the list item by item. Dimensions of the slot depend upon

[1] Each complete set will include about 6 lists (typewritten or mimeographed): 2 being lists of nonsense syllables, 2 being words in a nonsense order, and 2 being words in an order potentially meaningful. The lists should be given only letter (or other keyed) headings, by which they can be later identified. Examples:

Syllables (A, D)	Words, chance order (B, E)	Words, potentially meaningful order (C, F)
NIV	FOX	SUN
TEB	BOOK	WARM
DUT	SOUR	SAND
MOF	KIN	WAVE
LAK	HAT	BOY
		CALL

They should be placed in S's envelope in an irregular order so that the two lists of the same kind will not be drawn out in succession.

the printed lists used; and the length of the card should be sufficient both above and below the aperture to keep all the items covered except the one to be attended to. These dimensions should be previously determined and announced by I. Operating this sliding device with the left hand may at first be distracting to the memorizing: it should be well practiced on a preliminary dummy list.

When ready, draw from the envelope one of the slips of paper, and proceed to memorize the list printed on it in complete serial fashion by running the aperture of the card down to expose item by item. Practice until you are able to repeat to yourself the whole list in correct order without looking. Do not practice piecemeal (repeating a few items several times before reading others) but let each reading be of the whole series. (Why?)

Note the precise time required.

Follow the same procedure with the other lists, after brief rests.

C. (For both Individual and Group experiments)

At a later sitting, to be determined by the instructor, re-learn all six lists in the same manner as before.

Results and Discussion:

1. What differences are there with respect to subject matter between lists *A* (*D*) and *B* (*E*)? [1] Between *B* (*E*) and *C* (*F*)?
2. What is the order of difficulty in learning the different kinds of lists, expressed in time measurements? How does the difference between lists *A* (*D*) and *C* (*F*) [1] when expressed as a ratio compare with Ebbinghaus' ratio?
3. Show explicitly whether the learning had any of the trial-and-error character.
4. Compare the lists as to their effects on the learners' motivation (interest). Can you find illustrated in this case of learning either or both of the points made in the Dashiell text, bottom of p. 361 and top of next page?
5. What is the reason for the rest periods between the successive tasks? Seek several reasons bearing on this kind of work.
6. Does the order of difficulty (cf. 2 above) remain the same when tested for retention?
7. Do all your results on the retention test approximate Ebbinghaus?

References: Dashiell, 358–59, 360–64, Fig. 101; Woodworth, 74–80, 92–96; Breese, 254–57; Watson, 356–59, 362–65; Gates, 312–14, 329–31; Pillsbury, 380–82.

[1] I will announce the correct list-headings to be written in here.

XXXIX. LEARNING: SELECTIVE FACTORS (INDIVIDUAL OR GROUP)

Problem: To identify some of the conditions that determine which of several items will be selected in acquiring, and which of several learned habits will be selected in recall.

Materials: Several series of syllable-number pairs, *not to be examined beforehand*. Watch. Exposure device. Bell metronome or other timer announcing 5-sec. intervals.

A. Factors Operative in Acquiring

Procedure: (Individual method.) E must familiarize himself with the exposure device and should practice (without S's looking) presenting the successive items of the list through the aperture. Practice making the shift smoothly, and with good exposure, at each fifth second.

(Group or home method.) The individual student must serve as both E and S. He should place a card with a slit aperture in a position to cover all the items of his list. Then at each fifth-second signal he should slide it downward with his left hand to expose one at a time the successive items of the list. During each 5-second exposure he is to attend to the item or items being shown, as described in the following paragraph.

In the experiment itself, S is to attend closely. At each exposure in the series he will see a syllable and a number paired, and he should try to fixate the link or bond between the two by pronouncing them to himself. After 10 pairs have appeared he will then see exposed one at a time the same syllables as before, but in a different order and without their numbers. As each syllable appears S should try to write down the number that had been paired with it, making a dash line when unable to supply the number. Write these attempts to reproduce in a vertical row.

There are ten series in all. Two sets may be used when students work in pairs.

At the conclusion of this part of the experiment check your results with the original lists.

Results: Construct a table to show the number of correct associations recalled in each series, and falling under each heading:

Series	First associate	Last associate	Most frequent associate	Most intense associate	All other associates
I					
II					
(etc.)					

Total the number recalled under each factor and find its percentage of the total possible.

Results become more significant when averaged for the whole class, under directions of the instructor.

B. Factors Operative in Recalling

Procedure: Each S is provided with a blank on which appear simple arithmetical problems — not to be seen in advance! He is to attend closely to the directions to be given for each by I. (In the Individual form of the experiment, directions will appear on the blanks.) In all cases S should work *fast*.

Results: Compare your answers to identical problems, such as *I a*, *II e*, and *III c*; or *I b*, *II d*, and *III h*; or *I c*, *II h*, and *III b*; etc. Did the same stimuli arouse the same responses in all cases? But each stimulus-response association has been acquired as a habit in your past experience: then what special factor determines in each case *which* stimulus-response connection operates?

Discussion:
1. Formulate five laws covering the five factors that determine which of several S–R connections is most likely to be recalled, as brought out in this experiment.
2. In all these cases does "selection" mean intentional, conscious, deliberate selection?

References: Dashiell, 340–44, 370–72; Perrin and Klein, 82–88, 218–43; Watson, 314–16; Woodworth, 427–34; Hunter, 293–99; Gates, 281–83, 292–303; Breese, 243; Robinson and Robinson, 144–52.

XL. MEMORY: INDIVIDUAL DIFFERENCES FOR VARIOUS TYPES OF MATERIALS (Group)

Problem: Is "memory" a *single* trait?   Does one's memory capacity show itself equally for different kinds of materials?   To determine this by a comparison between the individual differences as found for different types of memory materials.

Materials and Procedure: A class experiment.   I will present various types of memory materials, differing widely in content, in manner of presentation, in subject's interests aroused, in method of reaction, etc.

Method of recording subject's reaction in each case to be announced by I.

Results and Discussion:

A. This is a selection of memory tests from a wide range.   To grasp their differences the more clearly, construct a table to differentiate them as to:

Sense modality used.   Items, whether single, serial, or paired.   Rote or meaningful material?   Special human trait tested?   Practical application as a test?   Etc.

B. To answer your problem:

(1) Score your own results on each memory test by I's suggestions.

(2) Determine your rank in the class results on each test.

(3) What amount of agreement do you find between your ranks-in-class on the different tests?

C. Find the intercorrelations (for the group) between the rankings on the different "memories," and arrange them in a complete table.   On the basis of the values of the table what memory materials would appear to have the most identical elements; what have the least?   What *are* some of these identities and differences?

References: Dashiell, 564–67 (and chapter xii); Perrin and Klein, 339–51; Robinson and Robinson, 762–67; Hunter, 88–91; Gates, 504–05.

XLI. THE AUSSAGE EXPERIMENT (Group)

Problem: Individuals differ greatly in their ability to give accurate testimony concerning an event that has happened within their own life-experience. The sources of error are many. They may roughly be divided into errors of original observation and errors of recall. Our problem here: to measure the degree of reliability of each student in observing and recalling memory materials presented by I.

Materials: To be chosen by I from the resources of the local laboratory.

Procedure: Having chosen suitable memory materials I will present them in a definite predetermined order. The members of the class, in the rôle of S's, will note them while they are being presented and will later be asked to make a report.

The report is to be obtained by means of interrogatories, I reading the list of questions and each S writing out his answers to them.

Results: After the reports have been made out, their inaccuracies are to be scored. I will dictate the correct answers, after re-describing the memory materials he had used.

1. Check the assertion that "the average reporter will make a score of about 75 per cent in accuracy, not counting omissions as errors."
2. Are there any "errors of insertion"? How many?
3. Are there any "errors of substitution"?
4. Are there any "errors of transposition" in time? In place?
5. If any items in the presentation had any emotion-exciting value, were they given more attention on presentation than were unexciting items; were they reported more accurately?
6. If I has used different forms of questions in the interrogatory, are there any errors due to suggestibility traceable to misleading forms (e.g., negative inserted into the question; an item referred to that was not included in the presentation; the definite article "the" used where an indefinite "a" or "an" is more appropriate; etc.)

Discussion:
1. Define a rumor in terms of the phenomena studied in this experiment.
2. The errors in a rumor tend to increase: do they probably increase in arithmetical, in geometrical, or in inverse geometrical ratio? Block out a possible experiment to attack this question.

References: Robinson and Robinson, 412–22; Gates, 393–94; Breese, 289–90.

XLII. PERCEIVING: VISUAL APPREHENSION SPAN
(INDIVIDUAL OR GROUP)

Problem: To measure the amount of material that can be perceived in a single act of attending, and to identify some factors affecting this.

Materials: Tachistoscope with short exposure, less than $\frac{1}{5}$ second. Printed exposure cards, numbered 1 to 10. (Cf. Dashiell, Fig. 67, p. 294.)

Procedure: E first familiarizes himself with the operation of the tachistoscope.

S prepares blank sheets for records, as described below.

At a "ready" signal S should look attentively at the center of the shutter hiding the card so that during the brief exposure of the card he can perceive as much as possible of the printed line. After each single exposure he should copy down what he has seen, using the second column.

For the individual form of experiment two sets of material are provided, A and B, A to be used with one student as S, B with the other.

The material consists of cards bearing different-length rows of crosses, digits, letters, words, sentences. (For the preparation of these cards, see note, page 98.) When about to show a new card, E should prepare S for the kind of material to expect.

Results: Prepare record sheets by ruling double columns, 2 inches to each column. Head them "Stimulus" and "Response," respectively. The number of record spaces needed will be announced by I. After the experiment copy the printed materials in the first of each double column.

State the greatest number of individual crosses, digits, or letters of each kind of material perceived by S.

Discussion:
1. The maximum span of perceptual attention is supposed to be how many unrelated stimuli? Compare your results with this, and make any explanation necessary.
2. How do you explain the different results with different materials? Be specific! What important principle of habit forming and learning bears on this?
3. Did S's eye actually "see" every printed character properly reported by him? How does this throw light on the "proof-reader's illusion"?
4. It has been said that "reading is a process of supplementation." Explain in terms of your experiment. Does this statement agree with the formulation on pp. 389 and 424 of the Dashiell text?

References: Dashiell, 293–95, 405, 415–17; Titchener, 287–90; Pillsbury, 273–77; Woodworth, 384–85, 389–92; Hunter, 308–12; Breese, 76–77; Gates, 375–76.

NOTE: Cards to be prepared in advance by I:

Set I bearing crosses in a horizontal row varying in number from 4 to 10;

Set II bearing letters in chance or nonsense order, 3 to 8.   (Some of these should bear the same letters as are used to form words in set IV, but here disarranged);

Set III bearing letters arranged in unfamiliar words, 4 to 12;

Set IV bearing letters arranged in familiar words, 4 to 12;

Set V bearing letters arranged in short sentences;

Set VI bearing heavy dots in nonsense scattered patterns;

Set VII bearing heavy dots in suggestive geometrical patterns (as domino patterns, "big dipper," chair, etc.).

Sets of type V can only with difficulty be used with the Group form of experiment, depending upon the type of tachistoscope used.   If types VI and VII are to be used students must use larger blank spaces for their reproductions and originals.

XLIII. PERCEIVING: THE MUELLER–LYER ILLUSION
(Individual)

Problem: To make a quantitative study of an illusion by the psycho-physical method of "Average error."

Materials: The Müller-Lyer illusion in single-line form adjustable by S. (Cf. Dashiell, Fig. 88*A*, p. 400.)

Procedure: S is to manipulate the adjustable card (showing Variable line). He should do this by sliding it carefully and gradually from the point set by E until the two segments of the long line appear exactly equal. (S must not slide the card back and forth when making the adjustment.) E is to take measurements of S's adjustments with a mm. scale, without the latter's knowledge of them; and he is to keep the record of these measurements.

A. Procedure Without Knowledge of Results

Start with the adjustable card to S's *right* and far out (when the right segment of the horizontal line will obviously be very much longer than the left or constant segment). S should slide the adjustable card *inward* gradually until he is satisfied that the two segments of the *horizontal line* look to him equal. (He should not do too much to-and-fro adjusting when near this point, but should try to reach it after movements in the one direction only.)

Note: S is to work honestly according to the way in which the line segments actually do *look* to him, regardless of whatever he may *know* *about* this illusion.

Repeat for total of:
> 5 trials *inward* from *right*.

Next, S should be started with the adjustable card in close, making the adjustable line very short. Then he should draw it outward gradually until the two segments look equal.

Repeat for total of:
> 5 trials *outward* toward *right*.

Repeat again:
> 5 trials *inward* from *right*.
> 5 trials *outward* toward *right*.

91

After a suitable rest, turn the whole figure about so that the adjustable card is to S's left.   Then, much as before, take 20 trials, as follows:

5 trials *inward* from *left*.
5 trials *outward* toward *left*.
5 trials *inward* from *left*.
5 trials *outward* toward *left*.

B. *Procedure with Knowledge of Results*

Let the two students change rôles as E and S; and let the S proceed exactly as did the other S, except that now he is to be kept informed of the amount of his errors.

S is to be given the first 20 trials with the adjustable card on the *right* side, in the order, 5 inward, 5 outward, 5 inward, 5 outward.   (The 20 trials with the adjustable card on the left need not be repeated by this S.)

Results and Discussion:
1. Does practice bring improvement to S in his efforts to overcome the illusion?   Does he completely succeed?
2. After making his 20 corrective adjustments on the right side, does S carry over his training to the task of adjusting from the left, or does the reversal of the figure bring back some of the original illusion? Consult your data.
3. Compare the mean (or average) and the average deviation for right- and for left-hand methods.
4. Did the knowledge of his errors assist the second S to overcome them, according to your data?
5. What are some theories that attempt to explain this illusion?
6. This method of determining a "threshold" is the Method of Average Error.   How might the procedure be changed to illustrate the Method of Limits?   To illustrate the Method of Constant Stimuli?
7. What *is* the "threshold" in this experiment?
8. Can you show how *Gestalt* is the important thing in S's perceiving?

References: Dashiell, 117, 399–400, 401, 408, 420–21, 563; Robinson and Robinson, 323–32; Woodworth, 412–20; Pillsbury, 329–39; Breese, 206–10, 222–28; Hunter, 318–20; Titchener, 332–38.

XLIV. PERCEIVING: VISUAL CUES AND THE THIRD
DIMENSION (Individual or Group)

Problem: The processes involved in perceiving a thing adequately may be many and extremely subtle. This is especially true of a person's perception of depth through sight. He seems, e.g., to *see* the distances immediately and directly, yet distances cannot be differentiated on the retina. (Why?) Your problem then is: To analyze out the visual cues that guide reactions in the third dimension.

Materials: (No special materials needed.)

Procedure and Results: (If done outside of class hours, first secure the coöperation of some one who will serve as your S in parts 1 and 2.)

1. Hold up before your S two pencils one foot and two feet respectively, from his eyes. Ask him to rivet his gaze on the nearer pencil, then on the far pencil. Now have him shift his gaze rapidly from one pencil to the other and back and forth as fast as he can. Do you observe eyeball movements on his part? Can he report any evidence of muscular activity in the eyeballs?

2. Have a card or book with large letters on it set at a distance from S. Have him keep *one* eye *closed*, and with the other gaze fixedly at one of the letters. Hold a pencil vertically about a foot before the open eye and as near as possible to the center of his line of vision without obstructing it. Now while his eye *remains focused on the distant point*, ask him to raise his arm straight over his head, then bring it down forward so as to touch his finger tip to the pencil point. Is his movement guided with accuracy by his (unfocused) eye? Have him change the focus from pencil to card and back and forth. Can he report any evidence of muscular activity involved?

3. (Using yourself as S) set up two books on your table, one with the flat side toward you and at a distance of two feet, the other book, preferably a thin one, touching it with its back edge toward you. The two books will form a T with its base pointing toward your eyes. Now hold the head in one position on a level with the books and open and close right and left eye alternately. Make drawings of what a camera would "take" in the two different exposures.

4. Find a position where you can look into the distance with a tree or some other object in the near foreground as well as one at a remote distance. Compare the near and distant objects analytically to determine what details would have to be used by an artist painting the scene to

enable a beholder to discriminate the near and far objects in his picture. Consider the following: Is the distant tree higher or lower in the 'picture'? Does the distant tree have more or less details? Is the distant tree more or less colorful (is it deep green or blue-grayish)? Is the distant tree larger or smaller in the 'picture'? Observing a particular clump of trees or a tree near a house, when one object partly 'covers up' another, which is to be taken to be the more distant one?

Discussion:

1. Make a list of the visual cues that guide reactions to near and far objects, and briefly state in what part of the experimental procedure each of these factors was shown.
2. Which of these factors are based upon present motor reactions? Which are based definitely upon past habits?
3. Which of the factors hold true for monocular vision? Which are found only in binocular?
4. Make a drawing of three trees supposed to be of the same actual size but at three different distances; name the factors above that must be recognized by the artist.
5. In general, what would you say as to the degree of *explicitness* with which these interpretative factors operate in influencing the way the organism distinguishes distances? E.g., does a person ordinarily call a tree distant *because* he has *noticed* its dimness, etc.... (Cf. Question 5 in the experiment, LOCALIZATION OF SOUNDS.) Are these true minimal cues?
6. What is the genetic explanation of the phenomena brought out in this experiment (i.e., why should such obscure details or characteristics of objects seen arouse in the beholder preparatory reactions of adjusting to near and to far distances)?

References: Dashiell, 387–89, 396–99, 411–13; Pillsbury, 314–25; Woodworth, 397–403; Warren and Carmichael, 151–60; Breese, 218–22; Titchener, 308–16.

XLV. PERCEIVING OF TIME–INTERVALS—(Individual or Group)

A. (Group method)

Problem: To measure a person's accuracy of time estimation as influenced by his occupation during the interval.

Materials: Stop watch. Metronome. Sheets bearing problems in multiplication or division.

Procedure: The S's are to occupy themselves with different assigned tasks during different intervals of time to be determined secretly by I. I will give the "go" and "stop" signals. S is to attend to the tasks and is not to try to estimate the time by counting, beating time, etc. After each interval is over, S is then to estimate its length, and record. When all the tests have been completed, I will announce the precise stimulus interval used in each case. S is to make his estimates under the following conditions:

(a) fatigue: at the "go" signal extending arms to the side with palms up and holding them there until the "stop" signal;

(b) hearing rapid metronome (about 184 beats per min.) started and stopped with the signals;

(c) hearing slow metronome (66 beats or slower);

(d) multiplying or dividing problems on paper or from the blackboard, as fast as possible;

(e) listening to an interesting story incident to be read aloud by I.

Results: Keep a tabulated record to show: stimulus intervals, response intervals (S's estimates), nature of occupations during stimulus intervals.

For each interval the estimates of the group members should then be averaged (or else, treated to show total numbers of individuals estimating greater, and less, than the true interval).

Discussion:

1. Considering carefully psychological differences in the "fillings," formulate any principles concerning their effects upon time estimation that seem warranted by the data (making explicit references to the latter).
2. Several investigators have found that women tend to make longer estimates of time than men: have you data on this?

B. (Individual method)

Problem: To measure accuracy of time estimation as modified by length of interval and by "filling."

95

Materials: Two simple keys. Kymograph. Signal marker. Tuning fork or other short time marker. Battery and wiring. Sound hammer or telegraph sounder. Metronome.

Procedure: Connect in one circuit S's key, the signal marker, the sounder (if used), and the battery. E's key is to be wired in contact with this circuit on each side of S's key.

Unfilled intervals. E sounds two taps, and after a short delay S is then to tap to mark off an equal interval of time. E should use such intervals as $\frac{1}{4}$, $\frac{1}{2}$, $\frac{3}{4}$, 1, $1\frac{1}{2}$, 2, $2\frac{1}{2}$, 3, 4, 6, 8, 10 sec. (as nearly as he can make them) 5 times each in irregular order. (For the longer intervals it may be necessary to slow down the kymograph.)

Filled intervals. E now fills some of the longer intervals between his taps with sounds from a rapid metronome (or some other "filling"); and S is to reproduce the interval by tapping (with metronome silent).

Results: The kymograph record is to be analyzed and the results tabulated to show: stimulus intervals, response intervals, and whether intervals are "empty" or "filled."

Discussion: What evidence is furnished by your data as to the truth of the following assertions:
1. "The relation of accuracy of time estimation to the length of the interval falls under Weber's law."
2. "There is a tendency to overestimate short intervals and to underestimate longer ones."
3. "Filled intervals are estimated differently from unfilled."

References: Dashiell, 413–15; Breese, 230–37; Pillsbury, 349–56; Robinson and Robinson, 298–306.

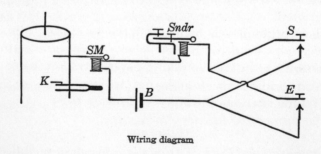

Wiring diagram

XLVI. PERCEIVING: EYE–MOVEMENTS IN READING
(Individual)

Problem: In reading do the eyes travel continuously along the line or make successive fixations? At what rates?

Materials: Eye-movement apparatus — a small mirror so mounted on a head band as to stand an inch or two in front of S's eye with its upper edge just below his line of sight and turned so as to reflect his eye-pupil to E looking over the shoulder.

Procedure: Adjust the head apparatus so that the top of the mirror is on a level with the lower edge of the pupil of the eye; thus S can look over the edge of the mirror to his reading material, while E can observe enough of the eye to note its movements. A little practice is required to catch the small rapid eye-jerks, and the method at best is a means to an approximate count. S is to begin at the left-hand end of a line and read naturally; E is to count the number of eye-fixations made to each line, and without taking his eyes from the mirror he is to jot down the number. (A frequent source of error is to count the eye-movements, instead of the *fixations*.)

After sufficient preliminary practice, S is to do his readings with different samples of material.

Results: For each piece of reading material calculate the average number of pauses per line; the average number of words per line; the average number perceived during one reading pause; and the number of pauses per second.

Discussion:
1. Was every letter of the print projected upon the center of sensitivity of S's retina?
2. The proof-reader's illusion was explained in part by a principle involved in the experiment on VISUAL APPREHENSION SPAN. (What was it?) What further principle of reading may be involved? (See text reference.)
3. Carefully describe each kind of reading material used, both as to typographical form and as to meaning. Then by comparison of them formulate statements as to the effect of each of the variables (or differences) on the rate of eye-fixations in reading.

References: Dashiell, 415–17; Pillsbury, 356–64; Woodworth, 357–59; Robinson and Robinson, 295–98; Warren and Carmichael, 281–82.

XLVII. SOCIAL PERCEIVING: OF FACIAL REACTION
PATTERNS (INDIVIDUAL OR GROUP)

Problem: Are the facial changes involved in different emotional reactions easily discriminated and recognized?

A. (Individual method)

Materials: Set of 24 photographs showing the same person in different emotional attitudes. List of names of emotions, shown below. Table of standard judgments of 100 subjects printed or posted.

Procedure and Results: Read through the list of words in order to refresh your memory with the names of different emotions. Turning to the pictures, observe them carefully one at a time (covering all but the particular one being used). Try to determine which emotion is most accurately represented or "expressed" by the pose in the picture. When satisfied, record your judgment by setting in a left-hand column the number of the picture and in a right-hand column the name of the emotion. (Limit your selection of emotions to the list given you.)

When all your judgments are recorded — and not before — turn to the list of standard judgments by the 100 judges. Under each picture number is to be found the number of times the name of each emotion was applied to that picture by the 100 individuals. Compare your decision on each picture with those in the standard list; and score it by writing after it the corresponding frequency number from the list. If no number appears for it in the list score it "0." What is your total score for the 24 pictures?

B. (Group method)

Materials: Large facial profile with changeable brows, eyes, nose, and mouth. List of names of emotions, shown below.

Procedure and Results: Setting up the profile in full view of the group, I will assemble various combinations of features to represent various facial reaction patterns. In each case, a short time will be allowed for the student to select from the list of names of emotions the one most appropriate to the face being shown, recording it opposite the number for that face.

The facial patterns will be assembled again in the same order; but this time I will name some emotion as each is being shown, and ask the student to judge whether that name fits the face "not at all," "poorly," "fairly,"

98

or "well." Each student will record in tabular form the number, the emotion named, and his judgment on the appropriateness of the latter.

I will now post the name supposed to correspond with each facial pattern (following the suggestions of Piderit), and also the various names for each that have been suggested by the members of the group, showing the frequency for each. Is there great or little agreement?

Is there any definite suggestion effect demonstrated by a comparison of the group judgments given after certain names were suggested by I with the judgments given before?

Discussion:
1. Do you think a person's thinking processes can be as easily read in his facial reaction patterns as his emotional responses?
2. What is the true psychological relation between emotion and its "expression"?
3. Do you think social life (in the broad sense) can have had any effect upon the tendency to emotional reactions in the face? Amplify your answer.
4. Do you think it at all possible to read the more permanent emotional and temperamental traits of a personality in the face? Explain your answer carefully. Compare this with reading traits by the shape of the skull.
5. State how the perceiving of facial reaction patterns brings out clearly the importance of configuration or Gestalt.
6. Make a list of those details of facial patterns you consider most important as cues in distinguishing the different "emotions."
7. Would you say that there was any difference between the dog and the cat in their ability to respond appropriately to the facial reaction patterns of human beings?
8. Discuss this general sort of technique as a "test of social intelligence."

References: Dashiell, 420–22, 427–31; Perrin and Klein, 161–71; Gates, 403–05; Hunter, 209–14; Woodworth, 287–91.

Modesty
Coyness
Coquetry
Contentment
Earnestness
Reproach
Shyness
Uncertainty
Yearning

Disgust
Repugnance
Dislike
Annoyance
Loathing
Aversion
Bored
Sneering
Scorn
Contempt
Disdain
Haughtiness
Superiority
Snippy, supercilious
Cynicism

Horror
Terror
Alarm
Fury
Frenzy
Fright
Passion

Suffering, physical
Suffering
Suffering, mental
Worry
Anguish
Despondent
Grief
Pain
Trouble
Sorrow

Suspicion
Antipathy
Distrust
Jealousy
Nothing
Timidity
Watching
Doubt
Self-abasement

Reverence
Religious
Religious love, faith
Aspiration
Adoration
Devotion
Humility
Prayer
Resignation
Suppliant
Trust

Fear
Anxiety
Dread
Expectation of disaster

Interest
Eagerness
Enthusiasm
Expectation
Hope
Want of interest
Amusement
Cheerfulness
Friendliness
Liking
Mediation
Romantic love

Vanity
Beauty
Bliss
Delight
Gladness
Happiness
Love
Pleasure
Playful
Smiling
Self-satisfaction
Desire

Tenderness
Sympathy
Pity
Comforting a child
Cajoling
Chiding
Love, altruistic,
    maternal
Pleading
Persuasion
Soothing

Laughter
Ecstasy
Glee
Merriment
Mirth
Rapture

Attention
Calmness
Calculation
Curiosity
Reflection
Sadness
Deep, penetrating thought

Amazement
Astonishment
Surprise
Wonder
Awe
Admiration

Determination
Assertion of will power
Bitterness
Displeasure
Defiance
Disapproval
Firmness
Hardness
Resolution
Self-assertion
Sternness

Despair
Dismay
Distraction
Bewilderment
Hopelessness
Perplexity
Racking brains
Thought

Anger
Hate
Hatred
Indignation
Dissatisfaction
Hurt
Irritation
Rage
Puzzled

Ugliness

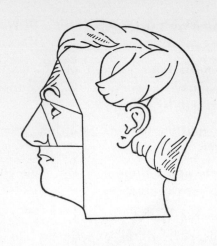

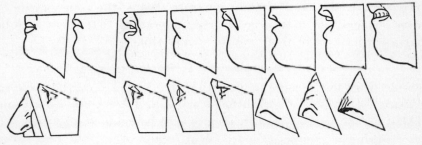

Facial profile model for Part *B*

XLVIII. SOCIAL INFLUENCES UPON INDIVIDUAL WORK
(GROUP)

Problem: To determine the effects upon an individual's work (1) of the mere presence of other non-competing workers, (2) of competition with others, and (3) of close observation by others.

Materials: Printed blanks for continuous work: multiplication, free serial association, mixed relations, etc.

Procedure: The individual is to apply himself to the same general kinds of work while in three different environments:

In Environment A (alone)

The student should do this part of the experiment alone. Several S's may work at the same time in separate rooms, the time signals being given by buzzers; but it is to be clearly understood that there is to be no comparison whatever of their results at any time.

In Environment T (together)

S should work in the same room with others engaged on the same tasks; but S's are not to look at each other's work, and it is to be clearly understood that no comparison of their results is to be made at any time. They are *not* working in competition to "beat" each other, but only to make good individual scores to be compared with their own scores on other tests.

In Environment R (rivalry)

S should work with others, but now on a competitive basis. The different individuals are now to try to excel one another. I will later call for all scores on *this* part of the experiment and will make individual comparisons to determine the fastest and most accurate worker, the next fastest and most accurate, etc.

In Environment O (observed)

Each S should work under the observation of others; the others are not to be working but are to sit near and openly watch S's pencil or pen. They should not see the material he is working on (each of them is later to use it); but they should keep their eyes fixed upon his pen and hand.

Results:
1. Each student will compare his accuracy or quality scores, and also his speed scores, on each test, with respect to the different conditions or environments. Which condition makes for most accurate work? Which for fastest work?

2. These results (cf. question 1) for all members of the experimental group should then be collected and assembled in tabular form on a blackboard, somewhat as follows:

Multiplication: Speed

	Highest	Second	Third	Lowest
A	(20)	(13)	(28)	(39)
T	(9)	..	..	..
R	(25)	..	..	..
O	(38)	..	..	..

Multiplication: Accuracy

	Highest	Second	Third	Lowest
A	..	..	..	..
T	..	..	..	..
(etc.)

(*Interpretation*: considering *speed of multiplication*, 20 individuals did their fastest work in situation *A*, 13 did their second fastest in *A*, 28 their third fastest in *A*, and 39 did their slowest work in *A*; 9 did their fastest work in *T*, 25 their fastest in *R*, and 38 their fastest in *O*.)

The group results are finally to be copied by the individual student as his final data.

Discussion:

1. Do the results for the group show that the mere presence of others is invariably facilitating as to speed? As to accuracy? (Cf. with Dashiell text.)
2. State *precisely* and *specifically* the differences in stimuli and also in responses: in *A* compared with *T*;
3. in *T* compared with *R*;
4. in *R* compared with *O*.
5. Suppose five subjects worked competitively under the observation of ten other people: where do you think the achievement of each would rank in comparison with results in *A*, *T*, *R*, and *O* situations?
6. Name one situation in everyday life similar to *A*, *T*, *R*, and *O*, respectively.
7. Are your quantitative results in this experiment as clear-cut in their significance as were those of such experiments as REACTION-TIMES or MEMORIZING OF ROTE *vs.* MEANINGFUL MATERIALS? Explain why as fully and as carefully as you can.

References: Dashiell, 436–37; Gates, 228–32, 238–40, 571–75; Perrin and Klein, 183–92; Hunter, 133–42; Woodworth, 258–62; Warren and Carmichael, 369–73.

XLIX. SOCIAL INFLUENCES UPON INDIVIDUAL OPINION
(GROUP)

Problem: The influence of others' judgments upon an individual's judgments is a fact widely recognized. Can such influence be measured? Is it of similar kind and degree in all fields of opinion?

Materials: To be supplied by I.

Procedure: Members of the class are asked to record their judgments between paired stimuli, taken from three different judgment-fields or categories.

(a) *Linguistic:* I will read one after the other a pair of slangy or ungrammatical statements or phrases. Each student will record whether the *first* or the *last* was the *more offensive,* F or L. So for a series of ten such pairs.

(b) *Ethical:* Similarly for a series of pairs of unethical traits.

(c) *Esthetic:* Similarly for a series of pairs of pictures, short tunes, or harmonic resolutions.

The record papers are collected.

On a later occasion, the experiment is repeated, but presentation of each pair of stimuli is preceded by I's statement as to what was the *majority* opinion on that pair. The student is to record the majority judgment in parentheses followed by his own judgment.

On a still later occasion, the experiment is repeated, I stating what is the *expert* opinion on each pair, to be recorded similarly.

Results: The student's papers are returned to him and he is to tabulate his judgments on the three occasions ("original," "majority," and "expert"). He is then to indicate whether there was a change of his judgment when the majority or the expert opinions were known ("change" or "no change"), and in either case whether his own judgment was (+) or was not (−) in line with those opinions.

Linguistic	O	M	E	Changes?	O–M	O–E
1	F	(F)F	(L)F		N+	N−
2	L	(F)F	(F)L		C+	N−
3	L	(L)L	(L)F		N+	C−
..					..	..
Ethical						
1	F	(L)L	(F)F		C+	N+
2	L	(F)L	(F)F		N−	C+
(etc.)						

All individual records are to be assembled in parallel columns and a copy is to be taken (from the blackboard or a mimeographed sheet) by each student, for analysis as follows:

1. Do an individual's judgments tend to conform more to majority opinions when known? In the same degree for all three categories?
2. Is the same true for expert opinions?
3. Are there any striking differences between individuals to be found in the tendency to conform to majority opinion? to expert? to both?

Discussion:
1. Psychologically, what is the meaning of "de gustibus non est disputandum"? Does it apply equally in all fields of opinion?
2. The tendency of the individual "to conform" has been ascribed to "instincts of the herd." Criticize this explanation, and offer your own.
3. Are your judgments responses to absent stimuli? In the same sense as in Figure 94 of the Dashiell text?
4. In the light of your experiment describe in objective psychological terms "mores," "authoritarianism," "martyrdom," "prestige," "fashion."

References: Dashiell, 258–60, 434–35, 446–48; Gates, 228–32, 238–40, 571–75; Perrin and Klein, 183–92; Warren and Carmichael, 361–66, 373–76; Hunter, 133–42.

L. ASSOCIATIONS BETWEEN IMPLICIT LANGUAGE
REACTIONS (GROUP)

Problem: "Our thought responses seem to come and go in a more or less connected fashion." What are some of the types of these connections, and what are some of the factors governing them? To show these by free and controlled association.

Materials: List of stimulus-words for Free association; list for Controlled association. Table of Types of association.

Procedure and Results:

A. Free Word-Associations

Prepare a paper for record by ruling off four vertical columns to be headed:

STIMULUS	RESPONSE	FACTOR	TYPE

Before opening to the page of stimulus-words, slip a card inside to cover the words and throw back the cover. When ready with pencil slide the card down to expose the first stimulus-word only. As soon as you see it read it by speaking it silently, and then as quickly as possible speak silently the first word that is suggested by it, that occurs to you — whether the connection is obvious or not. Then write both stimulus-word and response-word in proper columns of your record sheet. This done, slide the card down to expose second word in the stimulus list; and so continue until the whole list is used.

Now turn to your sheet of results and, inspecting carefully the first stimulus-response pair of words, decide what *factor of recall* was strongest and most operative in determining *that* particular association and no other. Name this factor in the third column. Have in mind: Frequency, Recency, Primacy, Intensity, Set, Context, etc. Continue in the same way with the remainder of your list. (Some find it easier to make this analysis after each response.)

Finally, try to classify the association involved in the first stimulus-response pair of words according to the following *types*. After deciding, record the name of the proper type in the fourth column. Continue in the same way with the remainder of list. *Great care* will be necessary here. Do not hurry!

TYPES OF ASSOCIATES

1. Contiguity in space, or in time — e.g., moon-star, lightning-thunder.
2. Similarity, or contrast — e.g., expensive-costly, summer-winter.

106

3. Cause-effect, or effect-cause — e.g., joke-laughter, injury-fall.
4. Whole-part, or part-whole — e.g., house-room, page-book.
5. Supra-ordinate, sub-ordinate, or co-ordinate — e.g., dog-animal, food-bread, pen-pencil.
6. Subject-verb, verb-object, or object-verb — e.g., dog-bites, build-house, deer-shot.
7. Substance-attribute, or attribute-substance — e.g., spinach-green, sharp-knife.
8. Rhyme — e.g., pack-tack.
9. Word-compounding — e.g., side-board.

B. Controlled Word-Associations

Prepare for records by ruling a paper into pairs of columns, long enough for 15 words each. Head the respective pairs according to the controls or types below, marking the first column of each pair "Stimulus," the second, "Response."

On each page of the booklet is a list of 15 stimulus-words. These are to be reacted to as in Part *A*, except that in each case the response-word must be one standing in a specified relation to the stimulus-word. Thus the words on the first page must be reacted to with their opposites. When ready slip a card under the cover, throw the cover back, etc., as done in Part *A*. Do likewise for the other pages of the booklet. When a stimulus-word and the appropriate response-word have been spoken (silently) record them both on your record blank, and proceed with the next word.

Five sets of stimulus-words are given; each set to arouse responses of a particular type. The types are: Opposites (contrast), Sub-ordinates, Verb-object, Subject-verb, and Attribute-substance.

Discussion:

1. Why are these reactions called "implicit reactions"?
2. How does your experiment show the associations of these to be much the same as for overt motor habits?
3. Can meanings be conveyed also by gestural reactions? Describe a few gestures for which gestures of opposite meaning can be given.
4. A natural science is interested in tracing cause and effect relations. Is psychology a natural science in this way as concerns implicit word responses? Does any such response occur to one without *any* causal basis at all?
5. Describe briefly some ways in which the association method of analyzing tendencies has been or may be applied for practical purposes.
6. How does the experiment on Controlled Associations demonstrate

107

higher order or general habits as well as lower order or particular habits? Give definite references.   How does it demonstrate the rôle of set?
7. Which is better found in revery, controlled or free associations?   Which is better found in working out the answer to a quiz question?
8. Both "factors of recall" and "types" (in *A*) have been called "laws of association" in the past; but which group seems to be more truly psychological or explanatory laws?

References: Dashiell, on implicit vocal reactions, pp. 480–85, 537–38; on the word-association method, pp. 221–23, 278, 545–46, 561; on factors of recall, pp. 340–43, 370–71, 394–96; Watson, 228, 346–49; Breese, 290–96; Warren and Carmichael, 278–80; Woodworth, 427–34.

LI. IMPLICIT SPEECH IN ADDING (GROUP)

Problem: (Student is to state it in full.)

Materials: Printed blanks bearing problems in addition.

Procedure: The blanks are distributed face down with tops toward the students. At a starting signal from I, all are to turn the papers over and to add the examples *as fast as possible*. At the end of 5 minutes or more, I will call "stop," at which all S's will mark the point reached in the examples.

Results: I may read off the correct answers; the group distributions in totals (columns completed) and in errors may be listed; and the individual S may compare himself with the group in both scores.

Discussion: In answering all of the following questions S must refer *explicitly* and *concretely* to parts or phases of *this* experiment.
1. Is the process of adding based upon motor speech processes? Overt or implicit or both? Show your evidences from yourself as S, from other S's about you.
2. As one adds cumulatively, is there any speaking to one's self or self-stimulation?
3. Is there any (implicit) behavior of the type called "serial," or at least a "train"?
4. By comparison of a trained adult's method of adding with that of a child first learning, point out how "short circuiting" is clearly involved in the former.
5. Are the responses of calling numbers "symbolic" responses?
6. List instrumental devices or methods that might be used to answer Question 1.

References: Dashiell, 347–50, 478–83, 530, Figure 59*B*; Watson, 343–56; Warren and Carmichael, 278–83; Woodworth, 442–45; Titchener, 521–25.

LII. DISCRIMINATING AND GENERALIZING
(Individual or Group)

Problem: (To be stated by student.)

A. *Visual Stimuli*

Materials and Procedure: E or I is to present a card (*A*) which S is to try to reproduce by drawing on his note-paper. The exposure time is to be short, and a number of such exposures is to be given, with an attempt at reproduction by S to follow each. S will record the number of exposures required for him to be able to reproduce completely the essentials of the figure.

Other figures (*B*, etc.) are to be presented in like manner; and the rate of S's improvement in apprehending and reproducing, from figure to figure, can then be determined.

B. *Auditory Stimuli*

Materials: Harmonium or organ keyboard, a number of organ pipes or tuning forks, or other apparatus for producing sounds simultaneously or in quick succession, in varying combinations.

Procedure: I or E will produce a combination of sounds to which S is to listen not as to a pattern but analytically. I will then produce a second combination; and S is to try to determine which of the component sounds was (or were) included in both combinations. I will produce a third combination; etc. S is to try to react analytically to the one (or more) identical stimuli in varying patterns, by sounding it aloud or silently, or otherwise symbolizing it to himself. This is to be tested by seeing whether S can react to it in a new combination or two.

Results and Discussion:

1. (*A.*) Does S's improvement, as measured by the number of exposures required on successive figures, bear any resemblance to learning curves? Of which type?
2. (*A.*) In S's various attempts at reproduction do his graphic responses show that he followed any consistent method: e.g., proceeding from a certain point in the figure; getting the general pattern and then working out the details, etc.? (Cf. Judd and Cowling, in the Dashiell text, pp. 407–08.)
3. Show carefully what phase of S's work in this experiment involved "discriminating"; "abstracting"; "generalizing."

4. In just what way does S's behavior surpass in achievement that of Strümpell's dog? that of Revesz's monkeys?
5. State how the experiment illustrates the law of dissociation by varying concomitants. Use the S–R formula to symbolize its meaning.
6. S has abstracted an identical element out of changing concomitants. Can one abstract a changing element out of identical concomitants? Illustrate.
7. Why was not the whole procedure to be followed in *A* described from the first, i.e., what is the psychological justification? (Cf. Hull.)
8. What is there in common between the phenomena studied here and others, such as, "selectivity in attending," "frequency as a principle of learning"? (Dashiell text, pp. 284 f., 340 f.)

References: Dashiell, 490–99, 501; Woodworth, 381–83, 392–94, 458–61; Robinson and Robinson, 534–37; Titchener, 529–40; Breese, 301–03, 308–12; Pillsbury, 417–22.

LIII. GENERALIZED RESPONSES: CHILDREN'S VOCABULARY
(GROUP)

Problem: To study the development of abstract and generalized meanings in the individual's behavior, by comparing children's verbal reactions at different ages.

Materials and Subjects: Lists of words.   Several children of different mental ages.

Procedure: Class demonstration.   The children are to be taken one at a time and asked by I to give the meanings of words named.   Students are to record all answers.

List I. Definitions.   "What does this word mean — (e.g., bread); what is — (bread)?"

List II. Similarities.   "How are these two things alike — (e.g., iron and silver)?"

List III. Differentiations.   "What is the difference between — (e.g., stone and egg)?"

Results: Go over your recorded responses critically and carefully.

1. Mark with *A* the responses given by each individual to List I, that seem to show emphasis on *action and use* of a thing; with *C* mark those that emphasize its *composition, form*, etc.   Then count up and tabulate them for different individuals.   Is there a clear difference here for the various mental ages?

2. Mark with *T* and then tabulate by number the responses of each individual to List II, that seem to show *trivial*, superficial, or occasional similarities (such as: both are the same color, same shape, you can't eat them); and, with *E* those that show *essential*, important ones (such as: both are metals, are heavy, used for making things).   What age differences are noticeable here?

3. Mark with *T* and then tabulate the responses to List III, that seem to show *trivial*, superficial, or accidental differences (such as: stone is harder, stones are red and eggs white); and, with *E* those that show *essential*, important ones (such as: stone is not edible and egg is, stone is not organic matter).   What age differences are there here?

Discussion:

1. Have you evidence to support the assertion that meanings are primarily motor and only secondarily become intellectual?

2. Terman says, "The ability to note differences precedes somewhat the ability to note resemblances" in individual development. Show whether your results tend to deny or confirm this.
3. "Generalized meanings are refined both by association and by dissociation." With an example from List II, show how association involves dissociation; with an example from List III, show how dissociation involves association (how one must assume some core of similarity before he points out a difference).
4. Write out a classification such as is used in a natural science or other field, to show how the names for generalized habits tend to fall into a hierarchy; and briefly point out how this is based on similarities and differences.
5. "A person's equipment of generalized reactions embraces those directed at different sorts of stimulating conditions." (Dashiell, p. 508.) Go over stimulus List I, and classify the words under the four heads mentioned after the passage quoted above.

References: Dashiell, 506–07; Woodworth, 451–61; Perrin and Klein, 293–303; Breese, 312–16; Titchener, 521–25.

LIV. THINKING: INDUCTIVE DISCOVERY (Individual or Group)

Problem: To test ability to grasp inductively principles of spatial arrangement, and principles of mathematical progression.

A. (Individual method)

Materials: Board with twenty-five insets; and set of disks. Lists of patterns. Specially printed record blanks. (As in Dashiell, Fig. 107, p. 517, but omitting numbers.)

Procedure: Arrange the board with the disks in the insets alternately black and white. S and E are to sit at a table opposite each other with the board between them. E is to choose one of the patterns in the envelope marked List *A*. He should not see those in List *B*! While S turns away, E is to hide a piece of brightly colored paper or some other suitable object in any one of the insets that is included in the pattern he has chosen. At the "Ready" signal, S is to turn to the board and proceed to hunt for the hidden object by lifting and replacing the disks one at a time. When he has found the object, he turns away again and E again hides the object. E should place it under another disk falling within the particular pattern he had chosen. S then hunts for it again. Trials are repeated until S's manner of hunting (or his oral statement) show that he has grasped the exact pattern. A second series with a second pattern chosen by E is then made; and so on for a total of five different patterns.

As S explores, E should record his progress on the blank by writing the numbers 1, 2, 3, etc., in order in the circles corresponding to the insets being explored. Use a separate record blank for recording each complete trial, labeling it with a letter denoting the problem-pattern and a number denoting the trial on that pattern. E should also observe the general methods of exploring. (See questions under *Results*, below.)

When the five patterns have been discovered, S and E should exchange places, the E now using the five patterns found in List *B*.

Results: Results are to be stated in terms of a description of the patterns used, and the number of trials necessary to discover each pattern.

Give as full a description as you can of the methods of exploration or search used by S. Consider: Does S ever lift the same disk twice in the same trial? Does he show a tendency to start at the same spot, or to follow the same course in successive explorations? Note any methods of exploration that you think indicate a rational attitude toward the task.

B. (Group method)

Materials: Yerkes multiple choice apparatus, with 6 volt DC current. (Cf. Dashiell, Fig. 106.)

Procedure: Have one member of the group serve as the S, all others to observe the performance fully, recording all presentations made by I and all choices made by S in each exploration.

S is instructed that I will set a problem of spatial relationship which can be found in successive settings or groups of keys he is going to push forward. S's task is to try to discover what that relationship is by hunting for the correct key in each setting: this key will sound a "buzzer." After choosing a certain problem, I pushes forward a few keys, their numbers to be promptly posted on the blackboard by an assistant. After a few seconds' delay (allowing the class to copy this setting), A is to begin pressing the keys one at a time until he finds the one that rings the buzzer. Class members must be on the alert to record each attempt made by S. When S succeeds in pressing the correct key first in 2 successive settings and can *also* then verbally formulate the relationship correctly, a second problem is set by I, using the same or a new S. Several problems may be used in the course of the group session.

Note: Part *B* is readily adaptable to an individual experiment.

Results: Each member of the group is to take his records in the following tabular form:

PROBLEM	SETTINGS	ATTEMPTS	FORMULATION
A	7–8–9	8, 9	
	3–4–5–6–7	6, 5, 3, 7	
	4–5	5	
	1–4–7–10	10	"first at right"

C. (Group method)

Materials: Blank with number series.

Procedure: DO NOT LOOK AT THE BLANK UNTIL YOU ARE READY FOR THE EXPERIMENT!

When seated with pencil or pen in hand, take the blank supplied. Read one line at a time only, and in each line write the two numbers that should come next on the dotted spaces.

115

Results: They appear on the blank.   (Were all series completed?)

Discussion:
1. "Induction" is often defined as the process of finding the principle or interpretation of a situation; "deduction" as the applying of the discovered principle to a new situation.   Show concretely how S's behavior (in *A*, *B*, or *C*) illustrates both of these.
2. Does inductive discovery follow a radically different method of progress than the learning of an act of motor skill?   Explain: In *A* or *B* how did S find the "answer" or principle involved?
3. Various hypothetical descriptions of the form in which an S does his thinking in such situations as provided in *A* and *B*, are offered in the Dashiell text, pp. 514–18.   Which of these seem to you probably most true of S's behavior in your experiment?
4. In *C* was there more or was there less random searching than in *A* or *B*?   What procedure replaces some of this searching?
5. Some leading characteristics of thinking behavior are described in the Dashiell text, pp. 521–30.   Illustrate each of these by a definite reference to something in this experiment.
6. (Adapt Question 5 from the experiment, PROBLEM-SOLVING.)
7. (Adapt Question 7 from the experiment, PROBLEM-SOLVING.)
8. Gestalt psychologists emphasize the fact that an animal is able to react not merely to the details of a situation in their absolute characters, but also to configurations or relationships that remain identical amid changing details.   Show how this is found in Revesz's work on chickens (Dashiell, pp. 401–02) and on monkeys (Dashiell, pp. 495–96) as well as in Yerkes' test (*B*).   But what additional psychological capacity is necessary for the latter?

References: Dashiell, 514–20, 521–30, 534–35; Watson, 349–56; Perrin and Klein, 243–54, 306–13; Woodworth, 149–51, 433–42; Hunter, 330–35; Breese, 338–42; Pillsbury, 427–30.

LV. THINKING: PROBLEM–SOLVING (INDIVIDUAL OR GROUP)

Problem: To study the nature of problem-solving by thinking in its essential characteristics.

A. (Individual method)

Materials: Healy-Fernald puzzle box. Watch with second hand.

Procedure: (Do not examine the box until ready to begin.) The box consists essentially of a glass door locked by a variety of simple mechanisms. When ready, E observes the watch, and S gives attention to the problem of unlocking and opening the door as quickly as possible. (This should be done behind a screen, if E is later going to act as S.) Use any way of going about it you think best. The buttonhook is for the manipulation of fastenings inside the box through the holes in the walls. No straining of parts is necessary! When success is finally achieved, E is notified, and the time taken for the whole performance is noted in minutes and seconds.

The box is closed and locked by the instructor, and the above procedure is repeated by the same S, after which he is to close and lock his own box.

S and E exchange places and proceed again as above.

Each S should finally write out a complete running report of his activities, overt and implicit, while working on the puzzle the first time. Consider: overt movements completed, overt movements only partially followed out, nascent starts of movement, sub-vocal remarks and formulations, sudden sniffs or grunts, changes in the direction of his visual attending. If the one who acts as E does not act as S he should take a copy of this report as given by the other.

B. (Individual method)

Materials: Tait labyrinth design on card. Blank sheets of paper. Watch with second hand.

Procedure: The labyrinth consists of a design that is to be copied by drawing one continuous unbroken line with no retracing of any part. (Crossings are permitted.) As S starts (working behind screen if E is later to act as S), E notes the time. S may examine the design as long as he pleases, time being taken from the moment he first sees the design until he finishes the correct drawing. As soon as S pleases he may try to draw the figure in the manner required. The original figure may be referred to while drawing. No attention need be paid to the technical excellence of the drawing: remember only that the line must be continuous and that there must be no retracing. If the first attempt is successful, take the time required; if not, observe the design and make new trials, until success comes, when E is notified and observes the time consumed.

After a correct drawing is made, E and S change places several times, until each student has made two drawings with a rest period in between. The time of each drawing is recorded.

C. (Group method)

Materials: Series of line puzzles drawn on charts or on the blackboard. Large clock showing minutes and seconds.

Procedure: The class is first given directions similar to those for B above. When all are ready and the precise time is noted, I exposes the first puzzle to view. The S's then individually attempt to reproduce it according to the directions. When S has finished he notes the clock again, and records the amount of time consumed in reaching his solution. He then reproduces the puzzle a second time, without seeing his first work; and records the time.

When one puzzle has been solved by all or most of the group a second one is exposed. (Those who have not yet solved the first should continue on it without looking at the second. When finally finished they should note the time, and shift to the second without waiting for a signal from I.)

A series of puzzles is to be presented in this manner. After the first one has been twice reproduced a second reproduction of each of the others may or may not be required, as I directs.

DO NOT READ THIS UNTIL THE EXPERIMENT IS COMPLETED!

Results and Discussion (answer briefly):

A

1. What time was required for each solution with the puzzle box?
2. Did S give the box a preliminary examination with his eye before attacking it with his hand? (How would a young child or an animal have gone at it?) About what fraction of the total time was given to this preliminary examination?
3. Did S's first attack upon the box prove successful?
4. Was S's final success attributable more to his hands' overt manipulation or to his implicit analysis of the situation?
5. Describe briefly the exact analysis used (e.g., tracing connections back

from lock, tracing forward from post for last cord, plunging *in medias res*, etc.). Mention also any unsuccessful partial analyses.

B or *C*

1. What time was required for each solution with the labyrinth, or puzzles?
2. How many drawings were required for each?
3. Was S able to see into the problem completely before attempting his first drawing? Was there trial and error here in any sense?
4. Was there finally an emergence of the correct plan "in a flash"?

General

Test each of the following principles by referring to the experiments:
1. The thinking mode of attack is economical of time and effort.
2. Careful attention to a problematic situation may lead to insight, to a sudden grasping of the essential principles in the situation.
3. An insight leads to immediate solution without a period of gradual progress, as in mere trial-and-error.
4. But learning by insight is only the trial-and-error method on a higher plane and with narrower scope.
5. "A complete act of reasoning...would include some five steps": maladjustment, diagnosis, hypothesis, deductions, and (sometimes) experimentation.
6. (If a series of puzzles was used by the group method.) "Transference of training is true not only for habits but also for insights."
7. (Ditto.) Show clearly to what extent the following processes were involved in your solution of succeeding puzzles: "discriminating," "abstracting," "generalizing."
8. (Adapt Question 5 from the experiment, INDUCTIVE DISCOVERY.)

References: Dashiell, 491–99, 511–13, 518–23, 541–43; Watson, 349–56; Perrin and Klein, 243–54, 301–03, 306–13; Robinson and Robinson, 518–19, 530–34, 543–45; Woodworth, 139–41, 433–42; Hunter, 330–35; Gates, 429–32.

Problem: (Student to state it.)

Materials: (None required.)

Procedure: To the letters A, B, C, D, E, F, G, H, I, and J, E is to assign the numbers from "1" to "10" in a random order (obtained from the instructor). He then calls out the letters in alphabetical order one at a time. S is to guess the number associated with each letter, E recording all guesses until the correct one is hit upon, when he says "Right!" (or merely calls out the next letter). E then calls the next letter, and so on. The series of ten letters is run over again and again until S can give each number correctly the first time, in two complete series in succession.

Several problems may be used, with E and S changing rôles after each.

(A preliminary experiment may be run using the five letters, V, W, X, Y, Z.)

Results: E will keep a record by writing across the top of a sheet the letters and the selected numbers for a given problem; and by recording under each the guesses made on each series. Thus:

	A 9	B 6	C 2	D 10	E 8	F 1	G 5	H 4	I 7	J 3	Errors L	P	U
First	3	8	5	5	8	7	10L	3	5L	3			
trial	5	7	3	7		5	3	7	3				
series	1	10	1	10		4	5	2L	7				
	2	3	7			1		6L					
	9	1	10					7P					
		6	9L					4					
			4										
			3P										
			2								5	2	24
Second	2	6	10	..	..	..	..	..	..	..	..	..	..
series	6		5										
	8		2			(etc.)							
	9												

The results on each problem are to be scored for — (a) the number of trial series necessary to satisfy the criterion of learning (two correct in succession); (b) the total number of errors of each kind; (c) total time. Errors are to be divided into the Logical (guesses that had already been used correctly for an earlier letter in the series), the Perseverative (repeating the same guess while reacting to a single letter), and the Unclassified. (When totaling errors, give double weight to L and P errors, triple weight to an LP error.)

E should plot 3 learning curves on one set of coördinates for each problem, using equal distances on the base line for the several trial series, and vertical distances for unclassified errors, total errors, and times, respectively.

Results for all individuals of a group should be totaled and averaged for the first two problems given each S (or one S of each pair). Using this class data, find what correlation exists between the problems I and II in unclassified errors; in total errors; in times; in number of trial series.

Discussion:

1. Are the individual learning curves plotted similar to those for acquisition of skill? Inspect carefully.
2. Is the learning on this test of precisely the same sort as learning by memorizing? Is it the same as learning by a sudden insight? Answer explicitly and fully.
3. Judging from your group correlations: which of the four criteria of learning efficiency is most reliable? Which least?
4. How would you go about determining the validity of this test as a test of general intelligence?
5. Comparing the procedures in 3 and 4, state clearly the distinction between the 'reliability' and the 'validity' of a test.
6. Peterson found this experiment, when used as a test, indicative of certain non-intellectual personal types of reaction-to-a-problem, including (a) cold rationalistic reactions, (b) extreme self-consciousness and emotional confusion, (c) rough hit-or-miss type motivated by abundance of energy poorly directed. How could the record sheets be made to reveal each of these types?

References: Dashiell, 511–21, 564–67; Perrin and Klein, 243–52, 306–13; Warren and Carmichael, 286–88.

LVII. SET OR DETERMINING TENDENCY (Group)

Problem: To identify some particular forms of set or attitude that operate as determining tendencies.

A

Materials: Printed sheets showing examples in adding, subtracting, multiplying, and dividing, in two types of arrangements. Stop clock.

Procedure: Each student is provided with a set of 4 sheets marked on the back, *A*, *B*, *C*, and *D*. He is not to look at their faces! When all are prepared the instructor will give the "go" signal and start the clock. S is immediately to turn over sheet *A* and to perform the simple calculations called for, working at top speed. When he has finished he should quickly note the precise amount of time taken to complete the sheet. This is to be recorded on the back.

Blanks *B*, *C*, and *D* are similarly used.

Results:

1. Which of the blanks shows fastest work; which next fastest, etc.? Show the times.
2. On which sheets was a given set longer maintained in the work?

B

Materials: Two sets of reading materials, each on four different topics. Each topic to be a short "story" (four to six statements) of fictitious history, of adventure, of scenic description, and of a scientific or political essay. In one set the statements will be combined all together in a circular order (one statement from the history account, followed by one from the adventure, then one from the scenic, one from the essay, a second from the history, etc.); in the other set the stories will follow each other as wholes.

Procedure: I will read aloud one of the sets of material, while members of the group (S's) listen attentively. At the conclusion they will be asked to answer a list of questions read aloud or furnished in printed form. Later, the other set of material will be read, to be followed by appropriate questions. If possible, the two sets should be used in reverse order for two halves of the class. (Why?)

Results:
1. On which set of material were more questions answered?
2. Point out any cases of interference between different stories. Are such cases more frequent in one set than in the other?

Discussion (*A* and *B*):
1. Could one say that response-tendencies may be in different degrees of readiness before any of them actually appear?
2. Frame a definition of determining tendency, involving your answer to 1.
3. "Determining tendencies in thinking are essentially the same phenomena as set in overt behavior." Comment on this, making reference to principles already learned concerning postural responses.
4. If possible, look up, define, and illustrate, "die Aufgabe," "die Bewusstseinslage," and "die Einstellung."

References: Dashiell, 281–84, 371–72, 527–29; Hunter, 287–89, 335–37; Warren and Carmichael, 300–01; Pillsbury, 284–85; Woodworth, 236–40; Breese, 353–54.

LVIII. IMAGERY (Individual)

Problem: Every student of psychology, even of objective psychology, should have had an acquaintance with introspective method at first hand. The study of imagery (or "mental images") is an excellent exercise: the introspective psychologist would recommend it as dealing with those aspects of the individual's private experience most clearly remote from any public or objective observation; the objectivist should welcome it as bringing to the student's attention those weaknesses in the introspective method he would emphasize. — Our particular problem: Can the individual analyze and describe minutely and accurately various imaginal aspects of his experience?

Materials: (No special materials needed.)

Procedure (*A*): Student is to act as both S and E. Sit in a quiet place and try to imagine yourself having the following experiences. Grade the VIVIDNESS of each experience on the following scale:

0. no image at all	4. vivid
1. very faint	5. very vivid
2. faint	6. as vivid as if object
3. fairly vivid	were present

In the first group try to have your experience in purely visual terms (try to "see" it), and grade only for visual vividness; in the second try to have the experience purely auditory (try to "hear" it); and so on. This will require great care as it is easy to confuse the modalities of imaginal experience. Do not hurry.

(1) Visual —
  a. A five-cent piece
  b. A street car
  c. Your bedroom as you enter
  d. A friend's face
(2) Auditory —
  a. An automobile horn
  b. The bark of a dog
  c. Your name being pronounced
  d. A familiar melody
(3) Olfactory —
  a. The smell of coffee
  b. Of freshly cut grass
  c. Fresh paint
  d. Old books

(4) Gustatory —
  a. Lemon tasted
  b. Sugar
  c. Salt
  d. Quinine
(5) Cutaneous —
  a. The feel of silk
  b. Of wool
  c. Of a pinch
  d. A pin prick
(6) Cutaneous —
  a. A snow ball in hands
  b. Ice cream on tongue
  c. Heat from a stove
  d. A hot potato in mouth

(7) Kinesthetic —
  a. Movements being made while shaking hands
  b. Climbing stairs
  c. Jumping
  d. Clenching fist

(8) Organic —
  a. "Feeling" tired
  b. Being "sick at the stomach"
  c. Being whirled around in a pivot chair
  d. Balancing yourself on hind legs of a straight chair

Procedure (*B*): Go over and repeat all the imaginal experiences called for in *A*, but now attend to their STABILITY. Grade them on the following scale:

0. no image
1. very fluctuating
2. fluctuating
3. fairly stable

4. stable
5. very stable
6. as stable as if object were present

Results and Discussion (*A* and *B*): Set down your results in a table, as:

IMAGE	VIVIDNESS	STABILITY
7 b	3	2
7 c	4	5

1. Average the Vividness ranks for the four experiences under each of the eight modalities. Then arrange a list of these eight modalities to show the general order of Vividness.
2. Proceed as in 1, but with reference to Stability.
3. Is there a high or low agreement between the grades for Vividness and for Stability in your results? Would you then say that these two attributes vary together absolutely, fairly closely, little, very little, or not at all?
4. Ascertain whether the order of vividness for the different modalities as found in your case holds true for the rest of the experimental group.
5. Your experiment has called for the imagining of concrete objects or actions. Do you think the imagining of abstract things would be easier or harder? Examples: "thoroughness," "multiplicity," "profundity," "astuteness," etc.
6. Do you think that the value and meaning of such terms as listed in 5 depends upon the vividness with which they can be imaged? Upon the particular form or character of the imagery?
7. Make a general comparison of your ability to describe (*a*) qualitatively and (*b*) quantitatively subject matter observed wholly subjectively (imagery) and subject matter observed wholly objectively (reaction times, psychogalvanic, memorizing, etc.).

Procedure (*C*): Some persons maintain that they have a clear visual image or "mental picture" of any word they are about to spell. If you are one of these persons try the following exercise; if not, find some one who is, to perform the exercise for you.

Take the fairly long name of some city or state, and get your "mental picture" of the name. Then proceed as fast as possible to call off the letters of the name in the usual forward (spelling) order. Next, proceed as fast as possible to call off the letters in the backward (reversed spelling) order.

Results and Discussion (*C*):

1. Were you (or was S) able to read off the letters from the visually imaged name in one direction as quickly and as readily as in the other?
2. If, when reading off the letters from the image in the backward direction, difficulties were met, what method did you find yourself adopting? Did you find yourself spelling forward at the syllable or letters where you were blocked and then resuming the backward letter-naming?
3. Make a careful and judicious statement on the topic: "The relative importance of imagery and of habit in spelling."
4. Eminent psychologists have debated whether "imageless thought" is possible. From your experiment what would you conclude about this? (Consider also Questions 5 and 6 under *A* and *B*.)
5. From the list in this MANUAL name three experiments in which all observations are made upon S by another person, E. Name three in which S was set to do his own observing and was to report this verbally to E to be checked with E's controls of objective conditions.

References: Dashiell, 11–12; Titchener, 197–200, 396–401, 505–21, 525–29; Breese, 238–40, 266–69, 271–74; Pillsbury, 254–64; Gates, 19–21, 416–23; Warren and Carmichael, 201–03, 217–20.

LIX. PERSONALITY RATING (INDIVIDUAL OR GROUP)

Problem: Any methods — even subjective ones — serving to identify traits of an individual-as-a-whole are of practical value, if their limitations are realized. Our problem: to observe some of the possibilities and the limitations in the rating scale method.

Materials: Blanks listing personal traits with numerical values for scoring each.

Procedure: One blank is to be used for self-rating. Follow the instructions on the blank conscientiously and honestly, trying to maintain an objective judging attitude toward yourself.

With the other five blanks five of the persons who know you well are to rate you. Put your name at the top of each. First make out a list of five persons whom you know intimately in many ways. (Consider: former or present teachers, schoolmates, business employers and associates, relatives who can be unprejudiced, etc.) Then mail (or hand) to each person one of the blanks along with a stamped envelope addressed as instructed by I. When all your returns are in, I will turn them over to you for statistical and psychological analysis.

Results: Construct a table to show: the estimates given by each of the five judges; the average and the A D of the five estimates on each trait; your own estimates. From this data plot a 'psychograph' to show your 'personality profile.' Down the left margin indicate the twenty-four traits, and by horizontal distances indicate the values 1 to 9. Then draw a heavy-line curve to show the average of the five judges' ratings, and light dotted lines to right and left of this to show the A D's. (Cf. Dashiell, Fig. 71, p. 320.) Using a heavy line of another color show your self-ratings.

Discussion:
1. On which traits is there relatively close agreement between the five judges? On which traits poor agreement?
2. Suggest explanations of the close and the poor agreements. (These may be the nature of the trait; the ease or difficulty of judging it; the circumstances or relations under which the different judges have known you; etc.)
3. Did any of the judges tend to rate you on all traits consistently high or low? Why, probably?

127

4. On which traits is there relatively close agreement between the ratings by you and by the others? On which traits poor agreement?
5. Suggest reasons for cases of extremely poor agreement.
6. Go over the list of traits and (by notations on your psychograph or on margin of a rating sheet) classify them under the five heads given in the Dashiell text: *A*. Intelligence; *B*. Motility; *C*. Temperament; *D*. Motivation; *E*. Sociality.
7. Is this an objective or subjective method of measurement? Which is the ideal of psychological technique? Explain why this method is used in this case.
8. Can you suggest objective methods adequate or nearly adequate for the reliable testing of any of the traits in your list?
9. Suggest several ways in which a carefully used rating scale of this general type may be of practical value. What dangers are to be avoided?

References: Dashiell, 551–56, Fig. 71; Perrin and Klein, 336–39, 364–75; Watson, 419–25; Woodworth, 556–63; Robinson and Robinson, 716–18; Gates, 405–09.

LX. PERSONALITY AND HANDWRITING (INDIVIDUAL OR GROUP)

Problem: Graphologists claim the ability to determine some of a person's personality traits from a study of his handwriting. Our problem is not actually to test this claim (which would require control of more conditions than are possible here), but to study the *methods or technique involved* in devising such a test. Two problems are involved: (*A*) what are the methods of determining traits of handwriting; (*B*) what are the methods of determining whether any relationships hold between these and traits of personality?

A

Materials: Ten specimens of handwriting for each student. Card with guide lines.

Procedure:

I. Judging by General Impression. Rate the ten specimens according to the *general total impression* each one makes on you. A good "hand" should be legible and beautiful, but do not think of these or other qualities separately: judge each sample by the way it impresses you *as a whole*. Place the best specimen at the left end, next best second from the left, etc. When satisfied with the ranking, record it.

II. Judging by Analyzed Traits. Mix the specimens again. Rate them with reference to the *five different criteria* or traits given below. Shuffle after each rating. (Caution: it is essential that when rating the specimens for a given trait you do not let your judgment of this trait be influenced by any of the other traits. Make each ranking an independent ranking.)

(*a*) *Uniformity of Slant.* No particular slant is required; but is the slant uniform (of the same angle) throughout? (Use the guide lines under the specimen.)

(*b*) *Alignment:* Do the letters come to a common base line: are the same kinds of letters of the same height? Etc. (Use guide lines.)

(*c*) *Quality of Line.* Is the ink line even in width, or evenly shaded? Is the line free from "shakiness"? Etc.

(*d*) *Letter Formation.* Are the "o," "a," etc., well closed? Do the last strokes of the "a," "d," etc., come to the base line? Are the last strokes of "b," "o," "w," etc., at a good height? Are "g," "f," "l" well looped: but "d," "p," "t," not looped? Etc.

(*e*) *Spacing.* Are letters joined with neither overlapping nor gaps?

129

Are words clearly separated? Are lines separated clearly but not too widely?

Results and Discussion: Make a clear tabulation of the ratings by General Impression and by Analyzed Traits (*a*) to (*e*).

1. Add the rankings in Analyzed Traits for each specimen: Does a definite total ranking appear? Compare this with the ratings by General Impression.
2. In your own judging were you able to avoid what Thorndike called the "halo" effect?
3. Try to state to what extent General Impression and Analyzed Traits enter into the rating of judges at a swimming-and-diving contest. At a livestock fair. Of an art or music critic. Of a state building inspector, or engineer inspecting a bridge. In picking an all-American football team.
4. How would you proceed to determine the relative validity of the two methods in the rating of, say, mechanical ability, or of general intelligence?

B

Materials: Lists of personality traits furnished by I, such as age, sex, intelligence, interest in detail, self-appreciation or pride, originality, aggressiveness, cheerfulness, and explosive *vs.* inhibited activity; with rankings on each for the ten whose handwriting was studied in *A*. (Some of these rankings may be based upon ascertainable facts; many will be a matter of personal judgment — as in the experiment, PERSONALITY RATING — on the part of I or others. But the validity of these rankings is not the problem here. It is: *Assuming* the personality traits ascribed to the writers to be true, what is the general *technique* for determining how they can be detected from their handwriting?)

Procedure and Results: In general, the method is that of seeking for correlations between handwriting traits on the one hand and personality traits on the other, by comparing the ranking of the ten individuals in each handwriting trait with their ranking in each personality trait, respectively. Work out coefficients for many or all possible relationships between them. Consider not only single traits of writing but also combinations. You will use many columns of figures: keep them all carefully labeled.

Discussion:

1. Age seems the most determinable trait from handwriting; do your data confirm this?

2. "The synthetic function of graphology is stressed at the expense of the analytic. The real measure of a graphologist's expertness consists in his ability to interpret signs in their relation to one another and to the whole complex in which they occur." Carefully discuss the bearing of this upon your experiment and results.
3. Relate the quotation in 2 to minimal cues and to configuration (in perceiving).
4. Do you think graphology belongs in the same class of "psychological gold bricks" with phrenology? Why? With other systems based on physical traits of hair, forehead, nose, etc.? Why?

References: Dashiell, 397–99, 420–22, 556–59, 564–67; Watson, 425–31; Gates, 405–09; Robinson and Robinson, 716–18.

APPENDIX

APPENDIX

NOTES FOR INSTRUCTORS

MISCELLANEOUS

Time for experiments: Most of these experiments are planned to take the greater part of a two-hour session. Where two consecutive hours are not available it is well to try to complete the experimental procedure in one period, data being left posted if possible; and then to analyze the results in another period. A few are short enough to be combined (e.g., those on Attending). On the other hand, some (e.g., Dissection of the Brain, and Social Influences upon Individual Work) require more than two hours time, and may be used for double assignment or may be cut.

Individual experiments: In most cases of individual experiments conducted in the laboratory the instructor should first briefly demonstrate the procedure on one student as S: it will save much trouble later, particularly in the earlier sessions.

Frequently three or even more students may use the individual form of experiment, rotating the rôles of S and E for the time allowed; and every one reporting at least one case.

Group experiments: Classroom demonstrations are in most cases admittedly compromises; and call for ingenuity in planning according to the particular local conditions. In some group experiments the groups cannot well be over 20–30 in number, and a much larger class would need to be sectioned.

In group experiments, where possible, every student should obtain his own data (as when he or a right-hand neighbor is S, or when readings on an individual S before the group appear on a large scale). Otherwise the results may have to be signaled to him, or posted on the blackboard for immediate copying. Kymograph records can be placed under clear glass, preferably over a ground glass plate illuminated from below, and posted in a convenient place for student tracing or analysis. In some group work a large clock such as the Whipple stop clock with a second hand visible to all is almost indispensable.

Reports: In some science laboratories, to reduce the opportunity for copied work out of class, the reports when finally handed in are placed on file instead of being returned to the student.

Paper materials: A great amount of paper materials, printed and mimeographed, is required for any extensive experimentation with large classes. Much trouble and vexation are saved by establishing rigid orderliness in the storing and handling.

135

APPENDIX

Every type of material should have its own container or envelope clearly labeled, or it should be kept in cabinets of pigeon-holed shelves, of about $8\frac{1}{2} \times 11\frac{1}{2}$ and appropriate heights, each shelf bearing a label holder and having a small arc cut out to permit ready grasping of papers by the fingers.

Batteries: In spite of their convenience in handling, dry cells are inferior to storage (preferably radio) batteries: the former soon give out and must be scrapped, while storage batteries can be re-charged at a service garage, or better by a rectifier, motor-generator, or other charger, with which a laboratory should be equipped. Batteries must have care if long service is to be expected. They should not be used to the point where they give out, as this injures them; and as they give out suddenly they must be carefully watched for water level and for strength as measured by a hydrometer. Terminals should be greased to avoid corrosion. Avoid using less than the three cells of a battery. To get lower voltages use a rheostat in series with one of the leads (taking care that the rheostat can pass the current without excessive heating), for using only one or two cells changes their relative conditions and may injure them on re-charging. Do not hook a battery with a low charge in parallel nor in series with one with a high charge. Voltages prescribed in the notes following may need changing depending on the instrument, contacts, length of wire, etc. Annunciator wire (double cotton covered #18 copper) is adequate for most routine work; and wire of the same gauge but with heavier insulation (e.g., fixture wire) can be used where it must be handled, rubbed, etc.

Kymographs: We recommend the kymographs furnished by the Harvard Apparatus Co. for most routine work. Extra drums are often desirable with each. The glazed paper should be fitted on the drum snugly, and the ends overlapped in the opposite direction from that in which the drum is to rotate, so that recording instruments will not catch in it. Recording instruments are always operated on the right-hand side of a kymograph (cf. Dashiell text, Fig. 58). Students should be shown how to smoke the paper-covered drums, how to handle them in recording, how to remove the paper by slitting with a knife edge slipped under it, how to draw the paper through the shellac-and-alcohol bath with forceps, and how to hang up to dry with spring paper- or clothes-clips. Ink recording, as used in polygraphs, is preferable to kymograph, but too expensive for routine class work.

Instruments: Ordinarily the instruments and materials referred to in this manual are obtainable from psychological, physical, and physiological supply houses, and can be found described and illustrated in their catalogues. In a few cases brief suggestions are made here for construction by local cabinet or machine works. When local construction is planned of pieces already on the market, it is recommended that at least one piece be obtained from a supply house to serve as a model. Indifferently made materials have a bad psychological effect on the student's attitude.

APPENDIX

Supply houses: The instructor should familiarize himself thoroughly with the catalogues of the first two supply houses named below. For many forms of apparatus it will be to his advantage to consult others as well.

Psychological:
C. H. Stoelting Co., 424 N. Homan Ave., Chicago.
Marietta Apparatus Co., Marietta, O.
E. Zimmermann, Leipzig.

Physical:
Central Scientific Co., 460 E. Ohio St., Chicago.
Gaertner Scientific Corporation, 1201 Wrightwood Ave., Chicago.

Physiological:
Harvard Apparatus Co., Back Bay P.O., Boston.
Max Wocher & Son Co., 19 W. Sixth St., Cincinnati.
E. Leitz, Inc., 60 E. 10th St., New York (also optical supplies).

Biological Models, Charts, and Slides:
General Biological Supply House, 761 E. 69th Place, Chicago.
Denoyer-Geppert Co., 5235 Ravenswood Ave., Chicago.
Chas. H. Ward, Rochester, N.Y.

Miscellaneous:
A. R. and J. E. Meylan, 552–54 Seventh Ave., New York (stop watches).
Sterling Stop-Watch Co., 15 E. 26th St., New York.
Beck Brothers, 121 Sedgley Ave., Philadelphia (rheostats)
Munsell Color Co., 10 E. Franklin St., Baltimore.
Milton Bradley Co., Springfield, Mass. (colors, paper materials, etc.).
General Radio Co., Cambridge, Mass.
Bausch & Lomb Optical Co., Rochester, N.Y.
Geo. H. Wahmann Mfg. Co., 520 W. Baltimore St., Baltimore (animal cages).
Leeds and Northrop, 4901 Stenton Ave., Philadelphia (electrical measuring instruments).
Edwards Brothers, Ann Arbor, Mich. (lithoprinting and mimeographing).

References: Every department should have for immediate reference all of the following:
Titchener, E. B.: *Experimental Psychology: Qualitative* — Student's and Instructor's Manuals. (Macmillan.)
Myers, C. S.: *Text-Book of Experimental Psychology* — Parts I and II. (Longmans.)
Whipple, G. M.: *Manual of Mental and Physical Tests* — Parts I and II. (Warwick and York.)
Schulze, R.: *Experimental Psychology and Pedagogy* (trans. by Pintner, R.). (Macmillan.)

These will be referred to in the following pages by authors' names only. Other manuals, and certain journal articles, that will be of direct practical help in setting up particular experiments will be mentioned in connection with the latter.

I. LOCALIZATION OF SOUNDS, p. 1

This is a good demonstration with which to initiate students into experimental methods in psychology. It is usable as a group experiment conducted by I even

APPENDIX

in an "individual" laboratory course. The problem is easily and interestingly introduced by reference to the fallibility of court testimony as to the direction of pistol shots heard, difficulties of pilots in responding to whistles and bells in fogs, etc. The exercise is a simple one, each detail of procedure being readily apprehended by the student; yet it is quantitative and can be used to direct attention to the need for precision.

Special references: Titchener, exp. XXXII; Myers, ch. XXI; Kline, L. W. and F. L., *Psychology by Experiment* (Ginn), exp. 73.

II. REACTION TIMES, p. 3

Sanford's vernier chronoscope is described by Titchener. It can be made up in quantities by a good mechanician by casting the base and uprights in one piece, attaching a pendulum clamp or inserting a brass rod for the cross-arm, then with a trout line suspending brass disks cut from bars, and setting spring paper-clips or telegraph keys for the releases. For C the Woodworth-Wells color naming test is used, as obtained from a psychological supply house (Stoelting). For D substitution test blanks can be purchased from a supply house or made up cheaply by clear mimeographing. We use digit-letter sheets showing in the code at the top digits $\frac{1}{2}$ in. apart with their corresponding letters placed $\frac{3}{8}$ in. below, and in the body of the sheet rows of digits in irregular numerical order about $\frac{1}{2}$ in. apart horizontally and a little more vertically.

Before every laboratory session I should have the pendulums properly checked with a stop watch for swinging rates.

Should it be desired to exhibit the operation of one of the more precise chronoscopes, a group experiment might follow in general the instructions for parts A and B of this experiment and part A of the following one, using an individual S before the whole group, and the members of the latter copying readings as they are posted by an assistant on the blackboard. There are several types of precision chronoscopes. The Hipp, operated by weight- or spring-driven clockwork, is the classic, but offers some difficulties of adjustment. The pendulum type is simplest in principle (models by Bergstrom, Hathaway, and others). The synchronous motor is utilized in Dunlap's model, which is standard in many laboratories (shown in Dashiell, Fig. 10). The galvanometer is utilized in Klopsteg's. Elaborate wiring set-ups that can be arranged with each make possible the study of many types of motor response to many types of stimuli. All are obtainable from psychology supply houses.

Special references (on individual A and B): Titchener, exp. XXVI; Schulze, ch. V; (on D) Whipple, test 37; (on C and D) Woodworth-Wells, "Association Tests," *Psychol. Monographs,* no. 57; (on group experiments) Seashore, *Elementary Experiments in Psychology* (Holt), ch. XVI.

APPENDIX

III. ATTITUDES IN REACTION TIMES, p. 7

(Cf. notes on preceding experiment.)

Special reference: (on *B*): Schulze, pp. 182–84.

IV. GROSS MUSCULAR FATIGUE, p. 9

In *A*, S must not advance his fingers on the stirrup beyond the first joint, and he must be reminded to pull his very hardest throughout.

Variations in the set-up of the apparatus may be used; the finger dynamometer may be used with a pointer to write directly upon a kymograph drum and so to graph the course of fatigue; the tapping board may be used with an electric counter as in the experiment, on MANUAL DEXTERITY. Best of all for the group demonstration, the ergograph may be used as illustrated in Fig. 15 of Dashiell's text; but the outfit is more expensive.

The finger dynamometer can be made in quantities by suspending a Chatillon spring balance (15 kg., obtainable from physics supply houses) from a wooden cross-piece supported on two steel bars about 2 ft. long bolted to a wooden base board. A rubber-padded stirrup is easily devised, as is also a movable kymograph pointer (when desired) connected by cord and pulley wheels to the stirrup and mounted upon a double-looped wire sliding between guides upon one of the vertical bars.

For a tapping board the writer has had screwed at each end of a 22 in. board a $\frac{1}{8}$ in. brass plate 4×4, with a binding post screwed through one corner for attaching the cord. The stylus, which must stand heavy duty, is a piece of $\frac{3}{8}$ in. brass bar 6 in. long, with an eye at one end for attaching the cord.

For signal markers, the writer recommends the use of the more substantially built (and higher priced) ones, wherever possible: the cheaper models supplied by many firms are frequently uncertain in action.

To secure time indications on the kymograph various means are available. The Jacquet chronometer is accurate and most convenient but expensive for duplication. The Lieb-Becker is satisfactory. Or, a simple signal marker may be used, in circuit with a seconds pendulum, a contact metronome, a Harvard electrical clock, or a vibrating spring interruptor. Several such markers can be wired in one circuit.

Special references: Schulze, ch. XI; Whipple, tests 9, 10; Myers, ch. XIV; Titchener, exp. XXIII; Howell, *Text-Book of Physiology* (Saunders), latest edit.

V. TESTS OF MANUAL DEXTERITY, p. 12

With practice I may be able to test a number of S's within a class hour, all results being posted on the board for analytical treatment at the next class meeting.

Smedley's hand dynamometer is recommended. Its type cannot be made up in quantity cheaply; but as it is used for only a few minutes by each pair of students, one or two instruments will suffice for a large number if passed around.

For electric counters in quantity, the "5-B message register" obtainable from the Western Electric Co. is recommended on account of its low cost.

For a coördination plate or steadiness tester the writer uses a $\frac{1}{8}$ in. brass plate $5 \times 8''$ bent in the middle at 90°. The holes are drilled with diameters given in Whipple, p. 157, and a Fahnestock clip post is soldered on the back. The stylus is fashioned of a stiff $\frac{1}{16}$ in. steel rod 5 in. long, looped at one end for attaching the cord and threaded through a hard rubber or wooden handle 4 in. long, leaving the wire exposed 1 in. from the point.

For *D*, tracing test, we use one of the blanks of the Hopkins series, preferably that one showing acute and obtuse as well as right angles and on the smallest scale. Obtainable from Penn Yan Printing Co., Penn Yan, N.Y. If preferred, the tracing test described in Whipple, test 12, can be used.

Special reference: Whipple, tests 6, 10, 13.

VI. WORK AND FATIGUE IN SEMI–IMPLICIT ACTIVITY, p. 15

E's reference number-tables should be worked out by I and mimeographed. Twenty columns of 21 numbers go easily on a page. Each column should begin with a two-place number selected in random order between limits of 10 and 29; and this should be followed below by the successive correct sums.

Examples:

18	23
20	25
23	28
27	32
32	37
34	39

(etc.)

The same sheet can be used over again several times if E is careful in the use of different markings.

Special references: Starch, D., *Experiments in Educational Psychology* (Macmillan), 1920 edit., ch. xvi, or 1913 edit., ch. xiii; Schulze, ch. xii.

VII. INTERDEPENDENCE OF THE ENDOCRINES: DRAWING, p. 17

This can best be conducted as a home exercise.

The student may ask I for further and more detailed information. The references below may be consulted. In any case, in a physiological field where physiologists disagree so greatly a psychologist need not hesitate to admit ignorance.

Special references: Timme (cited on p. 78 of Dashiell's text); Shäfer (cited in the same text, but to appear in later edition); Cobb, I. G., *Organs of Internal Secretion* (Wm. Wood); Berkeley, *Principles and Practice of Endocrine Medicine* (Lea & Febiger).

APPENDIX

VIII. CUTANEOUS SENSITIVITY: TWO–POINT DISCRIMINATION
p. 19

If needed this experiment can be performed as a group demonstration, using several subjects for comparisons. Care will be required, however, to maintain attentive attitudes on the part of the students; for merely looking on at a protracted exercise at threshold determination would not be an exciting occupation.

Special references: Whipple, test 23; Titchener, exp. 34.

IX. OLFACTORY SENSITIVITY: EXHAUSTION, p. 21

Special reference: Titchener, exp. XVIII.

X. AUDITORY SENSITIVITY: SOME TONAL INTERRELATIONS, p. 22

For producing difference tones, Young's difference-tone bars, Stern's tone variators, or (less successfully) ordinary tuning forks, may be substituted for the Quincke's tubes.

Special references: Titchener, exps. V, VII, VIII, IX; Myers, chs. III, IV.

XI. VISUAL SENSITIVITY: COLOR MIXING, p. 24

I would do well to draw on the board the color double-pyramid (Titchener, Student's Manual, Fig. 1) illustrating the Dashiell text discussion, pp. 109–10, and assisting the student to get oriented for this experiment. The pyramid should remain in sight or available during the experiment.

While not well standardized psychologically the writer has found the Milton Bradley cardboard disks more durable under clumsy student handling than the thinner paper disks furnished by psychology supply houses. For individual work many suitable types of motor rotators are obtainable from physics and psychology supply houses. A differential color wheel, permitting adjustments of disks while in motion (one shown in Fig. 34 of Dashiell's text), is, if substantial, usually very expensive; but it serves most admirably for group work.

Special references: Titchener, exp. I; Myers, pt. II, exps. 45–51.

XII. VISUAL SENSITIVITY: RETINAL COLOR ZONES, p. 26

The directions given are based on the use of a simple (Schweigger) type of perimeter, and are to be slightly modified if a more elaborate form (as illustrated in Fig. 35 in Dashiell's text) is used. Langfeld and Allport describe a procedure without a perimeter, to which our instructions can readily be adapted. If a group procedure is desired, one S is to be examined by I before the group, each determination being silently signaled or posted by an assistant for the group to copy. Several S's can well be examined and compared.

Special references: Titchener, exp. II; Myers, pt. I, p. 74, pt. II, exp. 52; Langfeld, H. S., and Allport, F. H., *Elementary Laboratory Course in Psychology* (Houghton Mifflin), 10–12.

APPENDIX

XIII. KINESTHETIC SENSITIVITY AND WEBER'S LAW, p. 28

Be prepared to lend aid to students if question 3 be assigned. Consult Myers. If the *A* method be used: we suggest obtaining empty shotgun shells and small shot; a cheap spoon with sides of the bowl bent up a little, and forceps, to handle the shot; cotton for padding the inner bottom of the shells; 1 set of accurate scales to the room, preferably the physicist's analytical balance, but the cheaper trip balance will serve. For Standard weights use, say, 25, 75, and 110 gr., with a variable Comparison for each. If the *B* method be used: we suggest making up weights of the materials mentioned above, or of wood, plugged and drilled, in the following sets: 100, 102, 104, 106, 108 gr., and 25, 25.5, 26, 26.5, and 27 gr.

Special references: Myers, ch. xv; Schulze, pp. 56–62, 83–88; Titchener, *Experimental Psychology: Quantitative*, exp. xxiii; Kline, L. W. and F. L., *op. cit.*, exps. 25, 27; Collins, M., and Drever, J., *First Laboratory Guide in Psychology* (Dutton), pp. 25–27.

XIV. CENTRAL FUNCTIONS IN THE NERVOUS SYSTEM: DRAWING
p. 31

This serves best as an exercise (or 2 exercises) to be done at home. The amount of detail to be required will depend upon I's emphases. (Erratum: Fig. 40 of the Dashiell text should show a synaptic break between incoming afferent nerve S_L and the nerve in the ascending spinal pathway.)

XV. DISSECTION OF THE BRAIN, p. 32

The instructions given are especially applicable to a head-with-brain model dissectible into 4 parts, the divisions being: brain removable from head, right and left halves parting at longitudinal fissure, upper and lower sections of right half, divided by artificial horizontal section. We use the Denoyer-Geppert model Y 13 or Y B 3a, but the instructions can be adapted to other simple models. An indexed wall plaque (we use Chas. H. Ward model 16b) and whole and sectioned natural specimens from an anatomy laboratory are of great aid to the student, as are also clear charts.

Prepared specimens of dog, cat, or sheep brain are obtainable from biological supply houses at moderate costs and sometimes from zoölogy laboratories; and can be used repeatedly. The sheep brain can be obtained from a local butcher, directions for removal of which are given in Fiske. The animal brain should be prepared in advance of the class work: it should be bisected completely in the plane of the longitudinal fissure, and one hemisphere should be further divided by a horizontal section. The students are to do no cutting or sectioning at any point. — The prepared animal brains are usually preserved in formaldehyde; and they are not to be handled much without prompt washing and, if needed, vaselining of the hands.

To prevent direct tracing the student's drawings should be demanded on a scale different from that of the diagrams or illustrations provided him; e.g., full size of the human model or twice the size for the animal specimens.

142

APPENDIX

Plates and diagrams covering the animal brains to be used can be provided the student by having the figures in one or more of the reference books listed traced on tracing cloth and then blue-printed, or photographed, or otherwise duplicated.

This is a long experiment, and unless cut it should be used for two laboratory periods of 2 hours each. However, students testify to its value in disabusing them of mystical preconceptions of the brain.

Special references: on human brain— Ranson, S. W., *Anatomy of the Nervous System* (Saunders); Lickley, J. D., *Nervous System* (Longmans), chs. III, V–VII; Howell, W. H., *op. cit.*; Ladd, G. T., and Woodworth, R. S., *Elements of Physiological Psychology* (Scribners), chs. IX–X; *on animal brains*— Fiske, E. W., *Elementary Study of the Brain* (Macmillan) (out of print but quite the best if it can be found); Reighard, J., and Jennings, H. S., *Anatomy of the Cat* (Holt); Mivart, St. G., *The Cat* (Scribners); Hyman, L. B., *Laboratory Manual for Comparative Vertebrate Anatomy* (University of Chicago Press); Howell, W. H., *Dissection of the Dog* (Holt).

XVI. REFLEX ACTION, p. 35

Both the knee-jerk apparatus and the winking glass are obtainable in certain models from psychology supply houses. They are somewhat expensive for duplication. For elementary work on the knee-jerk, we have used with some satisfaction a simple arrangement as follows. The hammer head is a light wooden block with one side whittled to an edge (not too sharp) and mounted on a wooden rod. The rod is swung freely from a suspension formed of a clamp (with hole opening) turning on a horizontal rod, the latter in turn mounted to the table edge (on which S sits) by a combination of rods and clamps. The amount of kick can be measured roughly, but with practice accurately enough for purposes of the experiment, by "sighting" the toe of the shoe against a chalk-lined floor from a constant point above the table: or, still better, by strapping to the ankle the lower end of a meter stick which is so pivoted to the lower corner of a board clamped vertically to the table top that the upper end of the stick will move across a scale drawn on the surface of the board. The latter feature is found in an inexpensive type of locally made apparatus described by Foster and Tinker (*q.v.*). (See figures accompanying student's instructions in this MANUAL, *supra.*)

A winking glass can be inexpensively devised — but with some expenditure of time — by setting up a piece of plate glass with support rods and clamps, in the figure, *supra*. All contacts of glass with clamps and wood base must be heavily padded; and no loose connections should be permitted anywhere, and all unnecessary noises eliminated. If preferred, the hammer can be struck by hand with a snappy wrist movement.

By rotating the E—S pairs, a few pieces of each of the kinds of apparatus will suffice for a large laboratory section.

Special references: Foster, W. S., and Tinker, M. A., *Experiments in Psychology* (Holt), exp. 2; Valentine, W. L., *Psychology Laboratory Manual* (R. G. Adams), exp. 1.

APPENDIX

XVII. THE CONDITIONED REFLEX, p. 39

Cf. figure accompanying student's instructions, *supra*. A saddle for the receiving tambour at the finger can be fashioned of cork and glued to the membrane. Trouble may be experienced in getting the registration of the reflex when made. A large tambour may be tried at the elbow instead of at the finger. Or, an electric substitute for the pneumatic tambour method is easily arranged, as follows. Place on S's finger a metal thimble to which a flexible wire has been soldered; put thimble and narrow finger electrode in circuit with a 2-volt battery and the coil of a relay; adjust the relay screws so that activation of the coil holds the armature against the insulated screw, and a break in the coil circuit allows the armature to close a circuit through a new signal marker replacing the recording tambour. Thus, any finger movement off the narrow electrode will produce a stroke by the marker. Electrodes may be of scrap pieces of sheet copper, tin, etc. We find that the narrow electrode should be on a level with the palm electrode, except when the hand is placed in the palm-up position, sometimes preferred. An adjustable wood elbow block and web or leather forearm straps will help to keep the reaction localized. (Cf. those on the ergograph, in Fig. 15 of the Dashiell text.) Students should be reminded that the C—R is at first somewhat diffuse (cf. the Dashiell text, p. 176).

For an inductorium we recommend that sold by the Harvard Apparatus Co. Double-contact keys, relays, and signal markers are sold by physics supply houses, signal markers and tambours by physiology and psychology houses, and miniature lamps, bells, batteries, etc., are to be found locally or at physics houses. A hand board with electrodes, receiving tambour and saddle, much as it appears in Fig. 52 of the Dashiell text, is sold by Stoelting.

In the course of the experiment I may need to readjust inductorium and rheostat. He should be ready to tighten screws on the secondary, and should watch the vibrator. Using a tetanizing current, S must have sufficient shock to establish the reflex. If the current through the lamp is too strong the rheostat should be adjusted, or, better, a shunt placed about the lamp.

A simple apparatus for the conditioned reflex experiment that has many things to recommend it has recently been described by Schlosberg and Carmichael.

Special references: Watson (reference given on p. 181 of Dashiell text); Barkley, K. L., *Jour. Experimental Psychol.*, 1931 (to appear); Collins and Drever, *op. cit.*, pp. 61–62; Schlosberg, H., and Carmichael, L., "Three New Pieces of Apparatus," *Am. Jour. Psychol.*, 1931, *43*, pp. 119–22.

XVIII. NATIVE PATTERNED REACTIONS IN ANIMALS, p. 42

For 1 and 2, we use wire screens of stiff hardware cloth, $\frac{1}{4}$ or $\frac{1}{2}$ in. mesh, about 12 in. square. For 7, the pan or tank should be at least 15 in. in diameter. The water should be at body temperature, and the animal should be dried on a paper towel immediately upon emerging. For 8 (*a*) a permanent floor may be built of

8 in. walls forming an alley 3 in. wide for about 15 in. of its length, the walls then spreading apart to form a 60° angle opening. For (b) a choice-point can be arranged by confronting the animal at the angle opening with an open-top 4 in. alley and a covered 4 in. alley, the cover being $2\frac{1}{2}$ in. above the floor. This can be done by modifying the apparatus used in (a) in a manner shown in broken lines in the figure: nailing or gluing $2\frac{1}{2}$ in. wood strips on the inner faces of the spreading walls, setting an angle of $2\frac{1}{2}$ in. pieces at the proper distance within the original angle, and covering one of the newly formed alleys with a wood or metal top transferable from one alley to the other. The students' work tables should be covered with paper for this experiment; and a lavatory with soap should be easily available.

A small animal colony is not expensive to maintain, once the original breeding stock of one or more dozen rats is obtained and the proper quarters are provided. Animals sold by the Wistar Institute of Anatomy and Biology, West Philadelphia, are the standard for all kinds of medical and biological research; but they are expensive, and most large cities or towns have animal supply houses furnishing white rats. For other animals I can reorganize the instructions.

Special reference: Greenman, M. J., and Duhring, F. L., *Breeding and Care of the Albino Rat* (Wistar Institute).

XIX. REFLEX PATTERNED REACTIONS IN CHILDREN, p. 44

Special reference: Schulze, pp. 154–62, 191–99.

XX. THE PSYCHOGALVANIC RESPONSE, p. 46

Different types of set-up are possible. The one shown in Dashiell's text, Fig. 60, II, is made more convenient if the Wheatstone bridge and the resistances are combined in one compact box. We use one with four dials ranging from 1 to 1000 ohms and a dial multiplying from .001 to 1000, shown in part of the figure accompanying the student's instructions. The Wheatstone bridge arrangement has the advantage of producing large deflections of the galvanometer, but the disadvantage of requiring frequent readjustments to the zero point. We use also the Godefroy tachogram set-up, employing a heavier current and a radio speaker-coupling transformer (either 1-to-1 or 2-to-1). This places the galvanometer in a separate circuit (secondary) from that of the battery and S (primary). The disadvantage of small deflections (requiring a large scale) is offset by greater convenience of operating. In this technique it is important not to make or break the circuit while the electrodes are on S, or a severe shock will result.

A galvanometer of a common type, such as shown in Figure 60 of the Dashiell text, is usable. It must be in a very stable position, preferably suspended on a wood block attached to a heavy wall. A lamp of the type sold with galvanometers should be used with it; and, if the group be small, a transparent scale. For a large group, a very large scale should be marked off with ink or crayon on white paper or sheeting,

APPENDIX

10 feet or more in length, to be mounted on the opposite wall of the room or hung from a pole suspended on support rods clamped to tables. Leeds and Northrup can furnish a specially built 10-foot scale.

For electrodes we use nickel plates 2 in. square, to the backs of which are soldered Fahnestock binding posts, held in place on the back of S's hands by adhesive tape. (These are not satisfactory for research work.)

Complete outfits for the PGR boxed in convenient cabinet form are to be had in the Hathaway and the Wechsler models.

As stimuli for part *B* we use such things as: odors (liked and disliked), loud noise, auto horn, threat to take off S's shoe, problem in 'mental' arithmetic, pin prick, threat of same, command to recite last verse of 'America,' to sing 'Sweet Adeline,' embarrassing questions concerning a 'petting party,' white rat placed on shoulder at neck, blindfold removed long enough to stimulate with flash of magnesium, etc., etc.

Special references: Wechsler, *Archives of Psychol.*, 1925, no. 76, esp. ch. IV; Landis and De Wick, *Psychol. Bull.*, 1929, *26*, pp. 64–119; Smith, W. W., *Measurement of Emotion* (Harcourt Brace); Collins and Drever, *op. cit.*, pp. 79–81.

XXI. CHANGES IN RESPIRATION AND PULSE IN DIFFERENT ACTIVITIES, p. 49

We recommend the Sumner pneumograph. For a sphygmograph we recommend a simple receiving tambour, easily improved by the use of two rubber diaphragms, as follows. When one has been mounted (with vaseline and rubber band or a cord), it should be drawn inward by suction on the metal tube, and the second diaphragm mounted over the bowl-shaped air-chamber thus created: when the suction on the inner diaphragm is finally released the air-chamber enclosed between the two will bulge out the outer one into a convenient cushion. — Diaphragms are to be cut from rubber dam, obtainable from dentists. — If difficulty is experienced in adjusting the sphygmograph to the radial artery at the wrist, it should be held by a steady-handed assistant against the carotid artery in the neck just under the jaw. — A sphygmograph of the air-chamber type described is sold by Leitz and others as a part of the equipment of the Mackenzie polygraph.

Special references: Schulze, pp. 124–49; Howell, *op. cit.*, latest edit.; Myers, pt. I, pp. 308–10; Titchener (Instructor's), exp. XXIV; Collins and Drever, *op. cit.*, pp. 77–78.

XXII. ORGANIC DRIVE, p. 51

The floor plan of the maze used by us is shown in the figure accompanying the student's instructions, with 4 in. alleyways. It is easily constructed of wooden floor and walls with a removable top of fly-screening stoutly framed. Lines should be lightly marked on the floor for the students' convenience in recognizing the squares. The maze may be unpainted with penciled cross-lines, or painted black throughout with faint white lines.

APPENDIX

For notes and reference on animals see the experiment, NATIVE PATTERNED REACTIONS IN ANIMALS. In this experiment it is important that the animals be frequently handled outside of their nest boxes for several days previous to the experiment. Unless they are thus accustomed to handling they will show a height of emotional excitement during the experiment which will obscure the effect of hunger on their behavior.

Special reference: Dashiell, *Jour. Comparative Psychol.*, 1925, *5*, pp. 205–08.

XXIII. ESTHETIC PREFERENCES, p. 53

The methods of entering records of the preferences should be carefully exhibited on a blackboard in advance, and demonstrated with a short series of objects not to be used in the experiment proper. The record sheets should be printed and distributed by I to save time.

For *A*, we use 20 geometrical designs as follows: 10 rectangles drawn to Fechner's vertical-horizontal ratios (1/1, 5/6, 4/5, 3/4, 20/29, 2/3, 21/34, 13/23, 1/2, 2/5), 2 right-angle and 3 equilateral triangles placed in various balanced and unbalanced positions, 2 parallelograms, 1 round-cornered triangle, 2 curved line figures. These can be furnished in sets of the 20 cards with a large reference card, by the Seeman Printery, Durham, N.C. (at about $8 per dozen sets). A variation that can be used is to have two colors mounted side by side on each card, for examining preferences in color harmonies. Poffenberger's set of 15 cards showing paired colors is obtainable from supply houses. For group demonstrations larger cards than either mentioned above will be required and should be made.

For *B*, we suggest the following intervals within the octave of middle C:

minor second	c d♭	fifth	c g
major second	c d	minor sixth	c a♭
minor third	c e♭	major sixth	c a
major third	c e	minor seventh	c b♭
fourth	c f	major seventh	c b
tritone	c f♯	octave	c c'

If I obtains a comparison set of data from young children they should be gotten by individual and not group testing.

(Erratum: Dashiell text, p. 104, interval C F should read 4/3.)

Special references: Haines & Davies, *Psychol. Review*, 1904, *11*, pp. 249–54; Gordon, K., *Esthetics* (Holt), ch. IX; Dashiell, *Jour. Exper. Psychol.*, 1917, *2*, pp. 466–75; Farnsworth and Voegelin, *Jour. Applied Psychol.*, 1928, *12*, 148–51; Titchener, exp. XXI.

XXIV. MOTIVATION: VOCATIONAL INTERESTS, p. 57

The administration of the test will usually consume between 25 and 45 minutes. The actual scoring by the student usually will take 20 to 30 minutes (exclusive of the time required to learn the method). It is then possible in two hours to give the test and have the scoring done for two vocations. Or, the test may be taken at home by each student (after preliminary instructions in class), and scored in class. If each individual is to score his own blank, there should be enough scoring scales on hand to supply each student with two. Some saving can be effected by exchanges between students after one scoring is done, but an ample supply of different stencils would permit a student to score for those two vocations that he claims as his first and second personal choices, which would add greatly to his motivation in this experiment.

In case the class is so homogeneous that the members may all be scored for the same professions, I could read out the weights for each item and the students write down their respective scores according to the way they checked the blank. A considerable saving would thus be effected in the cost of the scales.

Separate envelopes for each individual set of scales is a great convenience. Obtainable from Stanford University Press.

Special references: Strong, E. K., *Personnel Jour.*, 1929, *7*, pp. 441–54; Freyd (listed in Dashiell's text, p. 274), also, *Jour. Applied Psychol.*, 1922, *6*, pp. 243–54; Symposium on Interests, *Psychol. Clinic*, 1930, *19*, No. 2; Research Committee on Measurement of Interests, *Personnel Jour.*, 1930, *9*, pp. 176–83.

XXV. MOTIVATION: DETECTION OF HIDDEN CONFLICT, p. 58

Preliminary remarks to S are quoted in Dashiell's text, p. 221.

Somewhat more accurate timing can be made with a chronoscope and voice keys. (Cf. Dashiell text, p. 221.) We use a stop watch with satisfaction, starting it on the accented syllable of the stimulus word and stopping it on the first sound of the response word.

In the use of the sphygmomanometer a local physician can give advice. The Tycos aneroid (dial) type is most convenient. Obtainable from Wocher, from G. P. Pilling & Son Co., Philadelphia, or from psychology supply houses.

Special references: Münsterberg, H., *On the Witness Stand* (Clark, Boardman), pp. 71 ff.; Poffenberger, A. T., *Applied Psychology* (Appleton), pp. 488–93; Crane, Hull, Marston (references appearing on p. 227 of Dashiell's text); Tycos Blood Pressure Manual (Taylor Instrument Co., Rochester); *Instructions for Taking Blood Pressure* (American Institute of Medicine, N.Y.); Howell, *op. cit.*, latest edit.

XXVI. INFLUENCE OF EMOTIONAL DISTRACTION ON OVERT ACTIVITIES, p. 60

Modifications of the instructions used in the experiment, MANUAL DEXTERITY, may be made, especially as to time-intervals. For cancellation, ordinary magazine material is sometimes used; but we recommend more uniform material, such as the form mentioned in Whipple, p. 309, and furnished by Stoelting. Different letters

APPENDIX

should be used in different tasks. Noise is an excellent stimulus although under it the cumulative adding can hardly be checked for accuracy.

Special references: Morgan, J. J. B., *Archives of Psychology*, no. 35; Myers, pt. I, pp. 310–13; Titchener, exp. XXIII.

XXVII. MOTOR ATTITUDE IN ATTENDING, p. 62

The automatograph and its use are described in the Dashiell text, pp. 451–53. The smoked surface may be of glazed (kymograph) paper thumb tacked to a soft board. A pointer can be fashioned of light wire (such as the aluminum writing point supplied for signal markers) fastened with wax to the glass and bent over to ride lightly upon the smoked paper. As the ball bearings make an unstable platform E will set up and watch the instrument carefully. After the shellac-and-alcohol bath and the drying, the smoked paper becomes E's record; and in a group experiment it may be mounted under glass for inspection or tracing. Other details of procedure may suggest themselves to I.

Other forms of automatograph, ataxiograph, ataximeter, etc., obtainable from psychology supply houses, may be used.

Special references: Jastrow, Scripture (as listed in Dashiell text, pp. 452, 455); Kline, *op. cit.*, exp. 13; Titchener, exp. XXII; Myers, exp. 150, Seashore, *op. cit.*, p. 171.

XXVIII. FACTORS IN ATTRACTING ATTENTION, p. 64

The tachistoscope must be in good working condition. For individual work on this experiment we find satisfactory the Allport-Langfeld cardboard model with rubber band. For group work the Whipple disk type is standard, but care must be taken that the exposure cards can be seen by those sitting at the sides of the room. A very large class should be divided into smaller groups. For preparation and presentation of cards in set V consult Titchener.

Special references: Starch and Latshaw, *Experiments and Exercises in Educational Psychology* (Macmillan), pp. 190–212 (also in earlier edits. by Starch); Whipple, test 24; Titchener, Student's, p. 205, exp. 9, Instructor's, pp. 411–13.

XXIX. ATTENDING: SIMULTANEOUS ACTIVITIES, p. 66

Special reference: Whipple, tests 29, 30.

XXX. FLUCTUATIONS IN ATTENDING, p. 68

For group work the figure should be drawn on a large card.

Special references: Langfeld and Allport, *op. cit.*, exp. XVII; Starch and Latshaw, *op. cit.*, pp. 212–17 (also in earlier editions); Myers, pp. 318–20; Titchener, exp. XXV (3); Seashore, *op. cit.*, pp. 158–63.

APPENDIX

XXXI. INTELLIGENCE TESTS; INDIVIDUAL DIFFERENCES, p. 70

Some I's will wish to use this experiment early in the course in order to train students in statistical methods. I must remember that the average student does not readily grasp even simple statistical procedures until carefully demonstrated. A wide variety of tests should be selected (and mimeographed). We use: Analogies or mixed relations, Syllogistic reasoning, Writing from code (Terman's).

XXXII. JUDGING INTELLIGENCE BY APPEARANCE, p. 71

If the *A* form of the experiment be used, whether the work be done in the laboratory (individual) or in the class room (group), each student should be provided with a set of the pictures and later the list of I.Q.'s. They are inexpensive: obtainable from Prof. Rudolph Pintner, Teachers College, Columbia University, N.Y. They are best cut apart and mounted on cardboards with a letter to identify each.

If *B* be used, the children should be of the same sex and apparent age but of very different I.Q.'s. They can often be found in schools where a psychologist has recently made examinations. The children are to be given reference letters in a way clear to the class but not distracting to the children. The letters may be posted on a blackboard behind their chairs.

An excellent additional method of observing would be to have a snapshot group photograph of the children obtained earlier, and now projected on a screen before the children are seen in person.

Special references: Pintner, R., *Psychol. Review*, 1918, *25*, pp. 286–96; Gaskill, Fenton, and Porter, *Jour. Applied Psychol.*, 1927, *11*, pp. 394–403.

XXXIII. TESTS OF MUSICAL APTITUDES, p. 73

Full directions are given in Seashore's Manual, which is furnished with the disks as sold by the Columbia Graphophone Co., New York. It may be necessary to emphasize for the students both the manner of judging ("whether the second is," etc.) and the manner of recording. Much class time is saved by having the students' recording blanks printed or mimeographed in advance. Correct scores may be read off by I at the end of each test (which is more interesting to the student than if the scores are held until all tests have been taken), or inserted on a few of the scoring blanks and posted for the students to check by later. Distribution curves to be enlarged on wall charts will be found in Seashore's Manual.

Since this demonstration is a long one we have omitted from use the test of consonance, which is less reliable.

XXXIV. HABIT FORMATION: MIRROR DRAWING, p. 75

Several forms of mirror-drawing apparatus are furnished by psychology supply houses. Inexpensive substitutes are easily set up. Mirrors may be purchased at a ten-cent store and mounted with brackets screwed to the back. A screen is easily set up with a support rod and clamps holding fiber board. A cheaper substitute is provided by a piece of cardboard or stiff paper through which the upper end of S's pencil is punched, so that the screen rides on the pencil. Printed forms of stars are on the market, but once a plate is made they can be cheaply provided by a local printer.

Special references: Whipple, test 36; Starch and Latshaw, *op. cit.*, pp. 88–97 (also in earlier editions by Starch); Pyle, W. H., *Laboratory Manual in Psychology of Learning* (Warwick and York), pp. 39–46; Kline, *op. cit.*, exp. 81.

XXXV. HABIT FORMATION: MAZE RUNNING, p. 77

Many types of mazes are to be had of the psychology supply houses, their designs being shown in the catalogues. Mazes are quite inexpensively made by cutting out the pathway from fiber board on a band saw, and mounting it by nailing it flat to a smooth board. A single maze design may be drawn on paper nailed on top of several layers of fiber board, so that many mazes can be cut at once. With a single design four different maze patterns may be had by rotating the design, turning it over, and again rotating it. A stylus may be made by rounding off the ends of brass or glass rods about 6 in. long and of a diameter to fit into the maze groove without binding at any point. A guard to prevent the fingers from approaching too near the point should be provided in the form of a permanent flange in the material or a heavy rubber band tightly wound about the stylus about $1\frac{1}{2}$ in. above the point.

Special references: Kline, *op. cit.*, exp. 87; Dashiell, *Psychol. Review*, 1920, *27*, pp. 113–26; Foster and Tinker, *op. cit.*, exp. 14.

XXXVI. HABIT FORMATION: SUBSTITUTION, p. 79

This whole experiment may well serve as a double one, on a time basis. It will be more effective if more than 11 trials can be arranged. Separate reports on Results *A* and *B* are possible. The class should be divided by I into 3 groups (without advising them of the fact and certainly without the individual's knowledge of which group is his) to be supplied with 3 distinct sets of codes as hinted under Results *B*. For the final trial *all* students should be given a blank bearing a totally new code. The blanks with codes at the top can be mimeographed. (Cf. note on experiment, REACTION TIMES, part *D*.) The codes may be typed on separate small cards, making possible the printing of 1 set of the large blanks for all uses. The student can then hold the card with his left hand and move it down the page as he proceeds. Other methods of converting time and error scores into one score may recommend themselves to I. Some are given in Whipple, I, 312–14.

To clarify the description of the treatment of the 3 groups under Results *B*, the following sample codes are offered:

APPENDIX

	1	2	3	4	5	6	7	8	9	0
Suppose initial code to be	c	t	v	b	x	s	d	j	o	k
I group can be given										
for 2d trial	w	t	r	n	x	l	d	j	b	k
for 3d trial etc.	w	s	r	g	x	e	c	j	b	a
C group can be given										
for 2d trial	l	z	n	p	d	q	e	w	r	f
for 3d trial etc.	u	g	a	i	m	h	v	s	y	b

Special references: Dashiell, *Jour. Exper. Psychol.*, 1924, *7*, pp. 391–97; Whipple, test 37.

XXXVII. HABIT FORMATION: TRANSFERENCE AND INTERFERENCE, p. 81

Flinch cards are recommended since they provide more cards to the pack and as they bear larger numerals without distracting details. The two packs used alternately should be respectively of red and of blue backs. For pigeon-holes we use a framework built of $\frac{1}{4}$ in. stock to form 15 compartments $3\frac{1}{2}'' \times 5''$ and $1\frac{1}{2}''$ deep. A removable bottom adds tremendously to convenience in shuffling after a deal. Numbers cut from extra cards may be attached in one chance order to the inside backs of the holes as visible to S (lay-out *A*), and in another chance order to the inside fronts of the holes (invisible); the latter upon rotation of the framework then appear as the visible backs to form lay-out *B*.

Special references: Kline, *op. cit.*, exps. 85, 86; Pyle, *op. cit.*, pp. 52–62, 99–103; Starch and Latshaw, *op. cit.*, pp. 220–22; Dashiell, *Psychol. Review*, 1920, *27*, pp. 112–35.

XXXVIII. MEMORIZING: ROTE *vs.* MEANINGFUL, p. 83

The writer knows of no fully satisfactory very low-priced serial exposure apparatus. Some medium-priced ones, as the Kibbe or the Diehl type (Marietta), will serve the purpose. At this price level one might also consider the adaptation to laboratory needs of the "line-a-time" or similar commercially manufactured machine used by typists for exposing copy line by line, the adaptation involving only the attaching of a tall cardboard, fiber board, or metal screen with a properly cut aperture to the cross-bar line sighter. This has been improved in the Chicago laboratory, but the cost of the improved model is greater.

Special references: Whipple, test 38; Schulze, ch. VIII; Starch and Latshaw, *op. cit.*, pp. 146, 224–25.

APPENDIX

XXXIX. LEARNING: SELECTIVE FACTORS, p. 85

A. I should construct his own lists. (The Starch and Latshaw reference will aid.) In the even-numbered lists have one syllable-number pair printed in heavy characters to provide "most intense associate"; in the other five have a pair occur twice not in immediate succession to provide "most frequent." ("First" and "last associates" will, of course, occur in all lists.)

For group work have the students prepare their own (or furnish them) card or paper shutters, as described in instructions for MEMORIZING: ROTE *vs.* MEANINGFUL.

B. This part of the experiment must be conducted by I with discretion. Lists of arithmetical examples are to be printed (or mimeographed) in a form that would be equally suitable for adding, subtracting, or multiplying. See that certain examples are identical in the 3 lists to correspond with the first direction under Results. The following are suggestive.

I. Perform the following problems in arithmetic as quickly as possible, setting down your answers on this paper. *Note total time.*

a	b	c	d	e	f	g	h
18	20	13	15	9	..	..	..
0	5	7	5	2	..		

II. Perform the following problems, noting *time* taken.

a	b	c	d	e	f	g	h
15	18	9	20	18	..	..	..
5	9	2	5	6	..		

III. Perform the following problems, noting *time* taken:

a	b	c	d	e	f	g	h
9	13	18	30	..	..	..	..
2	7	6	10	..	..		

In conducting the experiment I should precede his start signal for each task by a general casual remark. Precede task I with some such statement as: "Addition is a process of uniting two or more quantities into one sum." Similarly, precede II with: "Subtraction is the process of taking away one quantity from another"; and precede III with a similar definition of multiplication. I will realize that he is not to tell the students in each case "to add," "to subtract," etc.; i.e., is not to apply his general statement to the particular case. The general statements may be printed on the blank just before the directions "Perform the following," etc., in the respective tasks.

Special references: Starch and Latshaw, *op. cit.,* pp. 146–70; Kline, *op. cit.,* exp. 62; Titchener, exp. XXXVII; Dashiell (text), p. 371.

APPENDIX

XL. MEMORY: INDIVIDUAL DIFFERENCES FOR VARIOUS TYPES OF MATERIALS, p. 87

I will use ingenuity in providing memory tests varying in as many ways as possible. For instance, we use:

Cursive designs shown on large cardboards (cf. Freeman, F. N., *Experimental Education* (Houghton Mifflin), pp. 189–90; Schulze, Figs. 219, 220; Kline, *op. cit.*, Fig. 39);

Madonnas — a series of prints shown, each accompanied by indication of the artist's name among several on the blackboard;

Connected discourse (cf. Whipple, test 39);

Melodies — the Seashore phonograph test for Tonal memory (cf. experiment, TESTS OF MUSICAL APTITUDES);

Color series — a series of patches of well-saturated colors on light gray card shown in a large serial exposure apparatus of the type used in the experiment, MEMORY: ROTE *vs.* MEANINGFUL;

Testimony — card of objects or picture (Whipple, test 32).

A large class will have to be divided into groups of a dozen or so if the working out of comparisons is to be done in class; or, the class scores can be posted on the blackboard out of hours for the students to copy and analyze at home; or, scores for a limited section of the class can be analyzed by the whole group.

Special references: Schulze, ch. XIII; Pyle, *op. cit.*, ch. XIII.

XLI. THE AUSSAGE EXPERIMENT, p. 88

As will be obvious, this demonstration should be presented a few days before the appropriate reading is to be assigned. We recommend the "event" type with more dramatic details than those used by Stern (for which consult references below, other than Whipple), and a formal interrogatory form of report (Whipple).

Special references: Whipple, test 32; Wigmore, J. H., *Principles of Judicial Proof* (Little, Brown), pp. 581–91; McCarty, D. G., *Psychology for the Lawyer* (Prentice-Hall), pp. 207–14; Münsterberg, *op. cit.*, pp. 49–54; Griffith, C. R., *General Introduction to Psychology*, Revised (Macmillan), pp. 515–23; Swift, E. J., *Psychology and the Day's Work* (Scribners), pp. 291–302; Gates, *Elementary Psychology* (Macmillan), p. 394.

XLII. PERCEIVING: VISUAL APPREHENSION SPAN, p. 89

Apparatus and procedure much as in the experiment, FACTORS IN ATTRACTING ATTENTION.

Special references: Langfeld and Allport, *op. cit.*, ch. XIV; Whipple, tests 24, 25A; Foster and Tinker, *op. cit.*, exp. 21.

APPENDIX

XLIII. PERCEIVING: THE MUELLER–LYER ILLUSION, p. 91

The simplest possible construction is to use two pieces of cardboard set in grooves. One piece should bear a horizontal line with arrow heads at each end of the line, one arrow head being at a tip end of the card. The other piece should bear a long horizontal line running from an end of the card to an arrow tail. If the latter piece be placed to slide smoothly under the former, the M—L figure is formed of one continuous line and three arrow heads (or tails) (as in Myers, pt. i, p. 288) instead of two separate lines and four arrow heads (as appears in Dashiell's text). For details of a fairly accurate but inexpensive construction of this type cf. Foster and Tinker. Several models are sold by supply houses.

For a still simpler construction, the "illusion of the vertical" may be used in either L or inverted-T form, with a slight adaptation of the instructions.

Special references: Foster and Tinker, *op. cit.*, ch. xii; Myers, p. 283 and exp. 141; Titchener (Instructor's), pp. 321–28; Judd (as listed in Dashiell text, p. 425).

XLIV. PERCEIVING: VISUAL CUES AND THE THIRD DIMENSION
p. 93

Special reference: Kline, *op. cit.*, exp. 71.

XLV. PERCEIVING OF TIME–INTERVALS, p. 95

In the group method I can use intervals varying not too greatly about some one measure: 1, $1\frac{1}{2}$, or 2 min. When working with filled intervals the individual S may be asked to estimate them in verbal terms instead of reproducing them by tapping.

For a rapid time marker a vibrating spring interruptor will serve in place of a tuning fork (Harvard Apparatus Co.). The Jacquet can be used if interval markings of $\frac{1}{5}$ sec. are small enough. The kymograph method can be avoided by using a stop watch and electrical controller; and with the longer intervals it would be accurate enough to use a stop watch alone, or even an ordinary watch with second hand.

Special references: Gulliksen, *Jour. Exper. Psychol.*, 1927, *10*, pp. 52–59; Myers, ch. xxiii; Collins and Drever, *op. cit.*, exp. 16.

XLVI. PERCEIVING: EYE–MOVEMENTS IN READING, p. 97

The apparatus is obtainable from psychology supply houses. For reading materials we suggest a wide variety with consideration given to size of type, length of line, interest, simplicity *vs.* abstractness of meaning, etc. A good variant is found in material run together without word spacings. A simple mirror arrangement is described in Starch and Latshaw, p. 48.

Special references: Freeman, *op. cit.*, exp. 9; Starch and Latshaw, *op. cit.*, pp. 45–53.

APPENDIX

XLVII. SOCIAL PERCEIVING: OF FACIAL REACTION PATTERNS, p. 98

For the individual experiment we recommend Feleky's pictures of emotions. These, with the table of standard judgments appear in her article; and are to be obtained from Miss Antoinette M. Feleky, c/o Teachers College, Columbia University. The table of standard judgments should be reprinted or mimeographed. For the group experiment, the Boring-Titchener model seems to be the only thing available. Full directions for assembling various facial patterns and their most appropriate names are contained in a reprint of the article by Boring and Titchener, accompanying the form sold by supply houses. Guilford and Wilke have described a modification of the Boring-Titchener, which can probably be used for this demonstration. The list of emotions printed with the instructions to the student is Feleky's; but it contains names identical with or closely similar to the twenty-four used by Boring and Titchener.

Special references: Feleky, and Boring and Titchener (references listed in Dashiell text, p. 455); Jarden and Fernberger, *Am. Jour. Psychol.*, 1926, *37*, pp. 565–70; Guilford and Wilke, *Am. Jour. Psychol.*, 1930, *42*, pp. 436–39.

XLVIII. SOCIAL INFLUENCES UPON INDIVIDUAL WORK, p. 102

If this experiment is too long it may be found advisable to omit environment *O* or even *R*. Unless many rooms are available for *A*, this may be done at home; but this necessitates each student's finding a person to keep *accurate* time on him in a separate room and to signal him with a tap on his door at the end of each interval. In any case, part *A* should not be done until the student has become familiar with the test and timing procedure in other situations, *T*, etc.

For mimeographed test material on $8\frac{1}{2}'' \times 11''$ sheets we use: "multiplication," 36 examples of 2-place by 2-place numbers with a line drawn below; "mixed relations," 45 examples of the analogies type selected from the standardized list of Pintner and Renshaw (*Jour. Applied Psychol.*, 1920, *4*, pp. 263–73); "free serial association," no special printing. Explicit instructions with an example is mimeographed on the reverse side of each sheet — the side the student sees before the start signal is given.

We sound a short buzz as a warning 1 min. before the first test; 2 sharp buzzes to turn the paper and start; 1 long buzz to stop and get ready for the next test, which follows in 1 min.

Special references: Dashiell, *Jour. Abnorm. and Social Psychol.*, 1930, *25*, pp. 190–99; Allport, *Social Psychology* (Houghton Mifflin), ch. xi.

XLIX. SOCIAL INFLUENCES UPON INDIVIDUAL OPINION, p. 104

I will prepare his materials in advance. Moore used: for linguistic, "everybody loves their mother," "she sort of avoided him," etc.; for ethical, disloyalty to friends, cheating on an examination, etc.; for esthetic, various resolutions of the dominant seventh chord played on a reed organ. For the latter, paired pictures of the cheap "Perry," "Copley," etc., type are a practicable substitute.

The three occasions involved would better be a week apart but if necessary they can be included in the same class hour. To the degree that memory participates, the character of the psychological processes studied is altered.

Special reference: Moore, H. T., *Am. Jour. Psychol.*, 1921, *32*, pp. 16–20.

(*Note.* For another exercise on social behavior cf. note to students' instructions on Experiment xxiv.)

L. ASSOCIATIONS BETWEEN IMPLICIT LANGUAGE REACTIONS
p. 106

We direct S to read his stimulus-word and speak his response-word silently because this serves to make more obvious to him the implicit speech character of the responses, although it necessitates provision of paper materials not needed in the usual overt speech method.

For stimulus materials in *A* we use 25 words of great variety typed on paper 3″ × 11″ and stapled at the top between cardboard covers made to hinge at the top. The cover is labeled "Free Association." For *B* we use 15 words suitable for each of the respective 5 types on 5 sheets of paper similarly cut and bound together with a cover labeled "Free Association." A blank covering card for controlling exposures is supplied within each booklet.

Special references: Kline, *op. cit.*, pp. 149–57; Woodworth and Wells, *op. cit.*, parts vii, ix; Whipple, tests 33A, 34.

LI. IMPLICIT SPEECH IN ADDING, p. 109

This demonstration calls for some skill in conducting, yet can be made a very valuable one, either as a formal experiment or as informal demonstration. For obvious reasons the Results may be omitted and concentration placed on the Discussion.

For question 1, I should — immediately after the adding test has been completed — raise queries as to how many heard their neighbor's whispering or other audible reactions; how many can recall whispering themselves or moving tongue or lips, or making counting movements with fingers, or breathing irregularly, etc., etc. Pointers that suggest answers to questions 2 to 5 can be gleaned from the Dashiell text references. The instructor should work out a systematic and concrete presentation of these points — to follow the students' efforts to work them out if assigned them.

We use mimeographed blanks showing many examples composed of ten 2-place numbers with a line drawn under each bottom number.

APPENDIX

LII. DISCRIMINATING AND GENERALIZING, p. 110

For *A*, cards are to be prepared with complicated geometrical figures made up of curves turned in varying directions, straight lines differing in length and direction, circles, dots, etc. — all assembled in serial, disjointed, intersecting, etc., manners. (The author will be glad to furnish a sample set on reduced scale.) A tachistoscope is not absolutely necessary to the individual method. Exposures of 2 sec. or longer can be made by hand as follows: Cover the exposure card with a blank card (or with the back of another card of the series), and expose it by lifting or drawing aside the covering card and then replacing the latter, by snappy movements. With a group, presentations of a figure can be repeated until all or nearly all can reproduce it. The exposure time is to be determined by I, depending upon the complexity of the figures, and should be set to require 3 or more presentations for good reproductions. Obviously, I need not give attention to questions 1 and 2. After the procedure as printed for the student has been completed, I or E is to continue by asking S or S's whether any identical segment in all the figures had been noticed. (*a*) S is asked to formulate or describe it in his notes verbally or graphically. (*b*) Then S is asked to identify it in a new figure or two to be exposed, in which all the elements (straight lines, curves, circles, etc.) are clearly lettered, and to record by letter in his notes.

If *B* is used, I should practice the presentation of stimuli. A pianist can pick out excellent combinations.

A good alternative experiment can be worked up with the analogies tests (with geometrical forms) included in such examinations as those of the American Council on Education, 26 Jackson Place, Washington. — Valentine has planned a more elaborate form of this general type of experiment for individual use in the laboratory, based on Gengerelli's research study.

Special references: Hull, Kuo (both listed in Dashiell text, p. 508); Gengerelli, J. A., "Mutual Interference in Evolution of Concepts," *Am. Jour. Psychol.*, 1927, *38*, pp. 639–46; Valentine, W. L., *Psychology Laboratory Manual* (Edwards Bros.).

LIII. GENERALIZED RESPONSES: CHILDREN'S VOCABULARY
p. 112

Get children of widely differing ages. Make each child at ease before the demonstration, and maintain an easy, natural, unhurrying attitude throughout. The stimulus-words should be distinctly heard by the class, and the child's responses should, if necessary, be repeated by I for their hearing and recording.

Sample words appear on p. 50 in Dashiell's text. The references to Terman may furnish suggestions as to procedure but his scoring methods are not strictly applicable.

Special reference: Terman, *Measurement of Intelligence* (Houghton Mifflin), pp. 167–69, 199–203, 221–31, 306–09, 324–27.

APPENDIX

LIV. THINKING: INDUCTIVE DISCOVERY, p. 114

The type of board and disks we use in A are easily made as follows. A certain cheap type of checker was bought in quantity at a ten-cent store; and these were glued and nailed together in pairs to form thicker disks. A piece of square pine about the thickness of a single checker was drilled with 25 holes slightly larger in diameter than the checkers, and was glued and nailed to another piece of wood (with grain turned at right angles to reduce warping), the whole board then being well shellacked.

The Yerkes apparatus for B is obtainable from psychological supply houses. If it is difficult to seat the groups where every one can see all the keys, an assistant should indicate S's movements by pointing at the key-numbers in the setting (already posted by him) in the order as tried by S.

Interesting problems for the inset board or for the Yerkes apparatus can be easily devised by I especially after noting those mentioned in the Dashiell text. The printed forms for the insets should resemble Fig. 107 in that text, but on a somewhat larger scale and without the numerals. I can make up the patterns for lists A and B of part A by coloring the appropriate circles on a few of the printed record blanks.

The mimeographed blank for C is of the type frequently used in group tests. Samples are given:

READ ONE LINE AT A TIME AND WRITE IN THE TWO NUMBERS THAT SHOULD COME NEXT IN EACH CASE

A.	2	3	5	8	12	17	..	..
B.	12	34	56	12	34	56	..	..
C.	24	27	28	31	32	35	..	..
D.	2	4	5	10	11		..	..
E.	2	4	12	48	..	..		
F.	16	17	15	18	14	19	..	..
G.	(etc.)							

BELOW STATE IN WORDS EXACTLY WHAT THE PRINCIPLE WAS IN EACH CASE

A.

B.

C.

(etc.)

Special references: Yerkes, Coburn (listed in text, p. 548).

LV. THINKING: PROBLEM–SOLVING, p. 117

The Freeman puzzle box, although more expensive, is preferable to the Healy-Fernald box. The former is more complicated and more interesting, and less subject to wear.

159

APPENDIX

Wire and other mechanical puzzles are not so good for the purpose as either of these boxes, for they usually arouse a disproportionate amount of manual manipulation and less thinking.

The Tait labyrinth may be found in either reference below. It should be drawn on individual cards.

For the group experiment we recommend the Tait labyrinth as the first puzzle, then a series of puzzles involving much the same type of problem and solution. Many may be found in puzzle columns of magazines. The author would be glad to furnish copies of a set he has assembled.

Special references: Freeman, *op. cit.*, pp. 34–40, 191; Lindley, E. H., *Am. Jour. Psychol.*, 1897, *8*, 461 ff.

LVI. RATIONAL LEARNING, p. 120

Special reference: Peterson, J., *Psychol. Review*, 1918, *25*, pp. 443–67.

LVII. SET OR DETERMINING TENDENCY, p. 122

Hints for constructing lists of examples appear in Dashiell's text, p. 282.

For related experiments cf. FACTORS IN ATTRACTING ATTENTION, V, LEARNING: SELECTIVE FACTORS, *B*, and ASSOCIATIONS BETWEEN IMPLICIT LANGUAGE REACTIONS, *B*. In devising the two sets of reading material great care is needed to equate them as nearly as possible before the statements of one are re-arranged in the circular order. The author can supply copies of sets used by him. When organizing the questionnaires consult Whipple's interrogatories; and as alternative to questions consider his method of scoring ideas in free reports.

Special references: (On methods of memory testing) Whipple, vol. II, pp. 23–29, 206–10. (For other experiments on determining tendency) Langfeld and Allport, *op. cit.*, pp. 96–97. Starch and Latshaw, *op. cit.*, pp. 182–86, 225–28. (On Discussion question 4) Titchener, E. B., *Experimental Psychology of Thought-Processes* (Macmillan); Boring, E. G., *History of Experimental Psychology* (Century); Warren, H. C., *Dictionary of Psychology and Cognate Sciences;* English, H. B., *Student's Dictionary of Psychological Terms* (Antioch College Press).

LVIII. IMAGERY, p. 124

Special references: Langfeld and Allport, *op. cit.*, exp. xxv; Seashore, *op. cit.*, ch. IX; Titchener, exp. xxxvi; Starch, *op. cit.* (1920), ch. VII, (1913) ch. IV.

LIX. PERSONALITY RATING, p. 127

The ratings should be anonymous and returned to I or to the department. In some situations I may find it necessary to send out the blanks to the judges himself, to prevent secret keying of the blanks by unscrupulous students. In such cases the students must be asked to furnish the instructor stamped envelopes addressed to the judges enclosing stamped return envelopes addressed to I or to the department. The burden of folding and enclosing the rating blanks, sealing, and mailing, is rather heavy.

We recommend the North Carolina Rating Scale, devised by F. H. Allport, copies of which are obtainable from Stoelting (#24511). The traits listed there correspond fairly closely to the list of personality variables in the Dashiell text, p. 552. We have followed the practice of mimeographing the following introduction and conclusion to a somewhat similar scale.

(Introduction) DEAR SIR OR MADAM: Students in the Department of Psychology are conducting a preliminary examination with special reference to personality traits in themselves; and they are seeking objective, unbiased judgments from persons they believe to be in positions to make reliable ones.

As a favor to the student named above — and to the Department as well — you are asked to follow the instructions carefully. (Several other persons are being requested to do likewise; and the student named will be furnished with no clue as to who is the judge making each of the respective reports.)

(Conclusion) Please mail (without signing your name) in the enclosed envelope at once, if possible, as it is urgently needed. If the envelope is mislaid, return this blank to Department of Psychology, Chapel Hill, N.C.

Special reference: Allport, *op. cit.*, ch. v.

LX. PERSONALITY AND HANDWRITING, p. 129

A makes a suitable experiment by itself, but may lack the extrinsic interest added by *B*. If *A* alone be used the handwriting specimens may be obtained from the members of the class by having each make out ten copies in ink, then distributing them. If *B* be used, I should obtain the specimens in advance (and permanently) from a chosen list of writers, varying greatly in age, in apparent (or better, tested) intelligence, about equally divided as to sex, etc. All specimens should be on unruled translucent paper. One phrase containing a variety of letters should be written by all. For the experiment furnish guide lines such as are provided with some writing tablets, or by ruling cards with neat India ink lines.

The traits in *A* and *B* are among those used by many graphologists. Quotation in *B*, 2, is from Downey, pp. 11–12.

An interesting variation is to secure handwriting specimens from several members of each of several families, and have students try to sort them into families. An excellent set of 12 handwriting specimens, accompanied on another page by personality sketches of the writers, is to be found in Norma V. Scheidemann: *Experiments in General Psychology* (Univ. Chicago Press).

Special references: Freeman, *op. cit.*, exp. 8; Downey, June E., *Graphology and the Psychology of Handwriting* (Warwick and York); Hull and Montgomery, *Psychol. Review*, 1919, *26*, pp. 63–74; Newhall, S. M., *Jour. Applied Psychol.*, 1926, *10*, pp. 151–61; Saudek, R., *Psychology of Handwriting* (Doran).